THE S…

Front Cover: Louis Callihoo at York Factory, 1842

Back Cover: Michel Callihoo at York Factory, 1842

THE SUN TRAVELLER

The Story of the Callihoos in Alberta

Elizabeth Macpherson

mhm MUSÉE HÉRITAGE MUSEUM

The Sun Traveller

Published by
Musée Héritage Museum
5 St. Anne Street
St. Albert, Alberta T8N 3Z9

Cover: Original Paintings by
Lewis Lavoie

Composition and Photo Reproduction by
Ingénieuse Productions
Edmonton, Alberta
Typeset in Hiroshige Book

ISBN #0-9694455-2-0

Printed in Canada

LIST OF PLATES

FOREWORD

Anonymity is the lot of most Natives in Canada. Historic records refer to Aboriginal People in the most general terms and many artifacts in museums have labels such as, "saddle, Plains Cree" and photos with captions like, "Father Albert Lacombe, with Indian friends." The purpose of this book is to put a human face on the history of one group of Native people in Alberta.

At the Musée Héritage Museum in St. Albert, the town's history is celebrated and the material culture of the original inhabitants is displayed. Many of these things belonged to or were made by people whose surname was a form of the name Callihoo. Especially intriguing is that the artifacts displayed include a Treaty medal. (Medals were given to First Nations leaders who entered into Treaties with the Canadian Government.) This discovery led to curiosity about the Callihoos and eventually the desire to tell the story of a family that includes both First Nations people and Métis. The first step was to find out who the Callihoos were. A genealogy was developed so that close relatives and more distant connections with other families could be studied. It turns out that a good many Native people in the Edmonton area are related to one another and that a great many families can trace their ancestry back to the first Callihoo and his colleagues in the fur trade. Thus, the social history of the Callihoo family reflects the experiences of many people of their time and place.

Members of the Callihoo family are mentioned in newspapers, scrip application records, court records, surveyors' records, journals written by clergy and books about Alberta history. Relatives and friends have their own stories to tell and many memories. Written records about the members of these families can be found in the Hudson's Bay Company Archives and in the Public Archives in Ottawa. There is some information at the British Columbia Archives and at the Glenbow Museum. The Provincial Archives of Alberta holds many records of the missionary order, the Oblates of Mary Immaculate. The value and quantity of the information are variable. Fur trade journals describe the daily life of the trading posts, but unfortunately the writers described little but the weather, the search for food and the maintenance and building work around the place. Names are rarely given, almost never of women or children, and social life is barely mentioned. The advantage of the information in journals is that they record each day's events as they happened. Many other writings are from memory and may be designed to make the author's point rather than to give just the facts. Financial ledgers give names of employees and the state of their finances but very little else. They tell of people's purchases, sometimes their jobs, and are orderly and probably pretty accurate.

Church records of baptisms, marriages and burials provide dates, ages and relationships. Here, women are mentioned as often as men. A little bit about personality emerges. One might infer, for instance, that Cécile, Michel Callihoo's sister, was religious or well-liked because she often acted as godmother to an infant, while his wife, Marie Savard, doesn't ever seem to have done so.

Newspaper stories have immediacy and are usually interesting, though they may be biased or inaccurate. Family stories are from memory and may also be biased. They may tell more about the person telling the story than about the subject. These latter biases are interesting just because the opinions are those of these very people.

The story is told in chapters mainly about each of three generations of Callihoos. There is an additional chapter about the Michel Reserve. The bibliography lists only those references from which both facts and ideas were taken. They are not always referred to specifically in the text. When referring to members of the Callihoo family in the main body of this study, one spelling of the name has been chosen. The term 'married' is used to refer to any union between men and women.

I want to thank especially Gilbert Anderson, Alice Callihoo, Beatrice Callihoo, Hector and Myrtle Callihoo, Napoleon Calliou, Paul and Octavie Callihoo, Richard Callihoo, Lena L'Hirondelle and the late Anne Anderson Irvine for the friendly way they allowed me to come to their homes and ask them so many questions. The opinions and errors, however, are mine.

Beside Highway 16, two and a half kilometres west of Spruce Grove is a sign erected by Historic Sites about the Callihoos and the Iroquois in Alberta.

Plate 1. Countryside, Michel Reserve, 1993
photo Elizabeth Macpherson

THE SUN TRAVELLER

Young Louis Callihoo came west to the Rocky Mountains nearly two hundred years ago. A romantic figure, he was described later as *le voyageur du soleil* [the sun traveller].

Louis was a Mohawk. He was born near Montreal and was baptized by a Jesuit priest on the day of his birth which was October 17, 1782, at the Jesuit mission village of Sault St. Louis, now called Ganawake. His parents are recorded as Marie Ann Tekonwakwehni and Thomas Anatoha (Kanakonme). The records also say: "Alla an Nord, sy maria, y eut famille, n'en revint jamais."[62] [He went north, married there, had a family there, never came back.] It is clear from this that he never returned, but someone who knew him did, and brought news of him. In this village, Louis learned his catechism and his prayers in his native tongue. He spoke French as well, which no doubt made his commercial dealings easier.

Louis was an adventurer at a time when there was very little government in the western territories. The fur trade companies exerted what few external controls there were. The resources of the land were exploited by people in defiance of geography in the form of muskegs, rivers and mountains. They also took on the extreme cold in the winter and the terrible biting insects in the summer. An individual had to be very self-reliant and competent to come into this environment from a more settled place and to prosper. Louis did. He also fathered a dynasty that consists now of more than two thousand people.

Northwest Company Engagé

It was customary to sign up in the winter to voyage in the following spring. And so Louis was hired at McTavish, Frobisher & Company, agents for the Northwest Company; contract #4582, on 23 November, 1800.[66]

[Translation of Louis' Contract]

Before the notaries of the province of lower Canada located in Montreal, the undersigned here present are Louis Caliheue of Sault St. Louis who voluntarily engages himself and is engaged by the here present Msrs. Mctavish Frobisher and Company. John Gregory, an associate, here present and being the one who accepts, for their first demand, to leave this city in the rank of middleman in one of their canoes to make the voyage so as to go up in order to winter for two years in the north and to come down in the autumn after the second year after wintering and going through Michilimakinac if required, carry eight Pieces [specific load of trade goods] over the Grand Portage upon entering and six Packs [specific quantity of furs] on leaving, or to reduce [take a loss of] six pounds or shillings in the old currency for each piece or pack, at the option of the 'Sirs' or their representative and to work six days at all other jobs, except carrying more loads – and having good and needful care on the trips, and having in place the merchandise, provisions, furs, equipment and all the things necessary for the voyage, to serve, obey, and execute faithfully all that the said 'Sirs' or all other representatives to which persons they may transfer the present engagement, will command him to be lawful and honest, to make their profit, save them from damage, alert them to information as he knows it and generally do all that a good servant must and is obliged to do without being able to make any particular deals, absent himself nor leave the service, under the penalties carried by the laws of this province and the loss of wages. This engagement thus made, unconditionally for the consideration of the sum of seven hundred in the first year and in the second, nine hundred pounds or shillings in the old currency of this province, that they promise to and are obliged to deliver, to pay to the said engagé a month after his return to this city, and on his departure double equipment. He acknowledges having received an advance on account of one hundred and twenty pounds and to receive on leaving sixty pounds in currency. He is obliged to contribute one percent of his wages for the Voyageur's fund. So in this manner etc. promising, etc. obliging, etc. renouncing, etc. ...

Made and concluded at Montreal in the chambers of the undersigned Notary, in the year Eighteen hundred, the 23 of November, in the afternoon, and signed with the exception of the said engagé who having declared he did not how to do it, made his regular mark after explanation was made.

Twenty words crossed out

This contract tells us something about young Louis' special skills: that he was hired mainly as a canoeman since he only had to carry packs to and from the main depot. He was expected to return to Montreal.

Generations of Iroquois had been trapping furs for a living and had become dependent on trade goods to maintain a comfortable lifestyle on the St. Lawrence River and in the Great Lakes regions. Did Louis go West because the populations of fur animals had declined at home? Did he feel stifled by the crowded village and the pressure of encroach-

PARDEVANT les NOTAIRES de la Province du Bas Canada, à Montréal y résidant, Soussignés, Fut présent *Louis Cahitomdiu Sault St. Louis*

lequel s'est volontairement Engagé et s'Engage par ces Présentes à *Mess. McTavish Frobisher & Co. John Gregory* un des Associé, à ce présent et acceptant, pour à leur premiere réquisition partir de cette Ville en qualité de *Milieu* dans un de leurs Canots pour faire le voyage, tant en montant *que pour hyverner deux années dans le Nord & Descendre l'automne après la seconde année suivant son hyvernement* et passer par Michilimakinac si il en est requis, passer huit Pièces sur le Grand Portage en entrant, et *six* Paquets en sortant, ou rabattre Six Livres ou Chelins ancien cours par chaque pièce ou paquet, à l'option des dits *Srs. Bourgeois* ou leur représentant et de travailler six jours à tous autres ouvrages, excepté de passer encore des pièces. ~~S'oblige d'aller au Lac de la Pluie s'il est nécessaire, en augmentant les gages ci-après de livres ou chelins~~, et avoir bien et dûment soin pendant les routes, et étant au dit lieu des Marchandises, Vivres, Pelleteries, Ustenciles et de toutes les choses nécessaires pour le voyage; servir, obéir et exécuter fidèlement tout ce que les dits Sieurs Bourgeois ou tous autres représentans leurs personnes auxquelles ils pourroient transporter le présent engagement, lui commanderont de licite et honnête, faire leur profit, éviter leurs dommages, les avertir s'il vient à sa connoissance, et généralement tout ce qu'un bon engagé doit et est obligé de faire; sans pouvoir faire aucune traite particulière, s'absenter ni quitter le dit service, sous les peines portées par les Loix de cette Province et de perdre ses gages. Cet engagement ainsi fait, pour et moyennant la somme de *sept cent* Livres ou Chelins, ancien courant de cette Province, qu'ils promettent et s'obligent de bailler, payer au dit engagé un mois après son retour en cette ville, et à son départ l'équipement *Double* reconnoit avoir reçu d'avance à compte *cent vingt livres et recevra en partant* s'oblige de contribuer d'un par cent sur ses gages pour le fonds des Voyageurs. Car ainsi, &c. Promettant, &c. Obligeant, &c. Renonçant, &c.

Fait et passé à Montréal en l'Etude du Notaire Soussigné, l'an mil huit cent le *vingt trois* de *Novembre* à *près* midi; et ont signé à l'exception du dit engagé qui, ayant déclaré ne le savoir faire, de ce enquis, a fait sa marque ordinaire après lecture faite. *Vingt mots rayés nuls*

(marginal notes:) *la premiere année et la seconde neuf cent livres* — *soixante livres de cours.*

+

John Gregory

L. Chaboillez

Plate 2. Louis Callihoo's contract with the Northwest Company,
Montreal, November 23,1800
courtesy Quebec Provincial Archives

ing 'civilization'? Perhaps this teenager was tempted by the salary, the clothes and the other items that were part of the outfit for company employees or *engagés*. Or was it his adventurous spirit that led this young man to leave his family to travel west with the sun? He had just turned eighteen when he became a member of an enormous continental enterprise.

Duly engaged, Louis Callihoo made the long and arduous canoe journey to the West as a voyageur. The Northwest Company hired mostly French-speaking labourers from Lower Canada although the partners and governors were mostly British. The traders and clerks tended to be Englishmen, Scotsmen and even some Americans. Colin Robertson, a fur trader, said he preferred the Iroquois to French-Canadians in a rapid or dangerous river crossing, "for their calmness and presence of mind which never forsakes them in the greatest danger."[75] The "servants," known nowadays as 'voyageurs', were for the most part illiterate and the language normally used was French. Of all the hired servants at Lesser Slave Lake, one Iroquois was said to be able to read and write.[4] Could this have been Joseph Gray (Louis' son-in-law)? There were Algonkian and Ojibway, as well as Iroquois, amongst the voyageurs. A list of Northwest Company

---

The name Callihoo no doubt comes from "Karhioo," which is an Iroquois name. It is thought by some that it means 'tall forest'. Louis also went by the name L'Iroquois as did many other compatriots. Another name that people wrote down as a surname for Louis was the name, Kwarakwante, or Karaconti, sometimes spelled Karaquienthe, and Caraquanti. This is a woman's name. We can suppose that he remarked that he was descended from a lady of this name. Many members of the family, especially from the West, had the name Karakonti bestowed on them by the clergy from the first. There was also an Ignace Kwarakwante in the mountain area who is said by some to be Louis' brother or cousin. He does not appear to have signed up in Montreal with the Northwest Company but must have come west by some other means or signed on elsewhere. There was also a Bernard Karakonti who apparently never married and was around 100 years old when he died in St. Albert in 1896. Some fur traders or priests spelt Louis' other name Calihue, Caliheue, Caleha, Calehoe, Collio, Calliot, Kalliou, Calistrois and Calehuis. There are those who believe that it was Father Lacombe who bestowed the name on the family some forty years later, from the French word, *caillow* but the priest wasn't even born when Louis signed his first contract. Now that everyone can read and write, some families have chosen to spell their names Calahoo, Callioux, Calliou, Callihoe, Calihoo, or Callihoo. In this book, the last spelling is used throughout for clarity.

servants for 1805 even includes a "Negro" called Pierre Bonga. At any one time, there might have been as many as a thousand employees of different ranks in the Northwest Company service.

Before trading posts could be built and manned, exploration and mapping of the hinterland was done with men or even women native to the region hired as guides. Explorers went out into the wilderness to look for groups of people who would bring furs and food to trade and they also had to find good transportation routes. David Thompson was one of the most important explorers for the Northwest Company in the regions we now call British Columbia and Alberta. Some of the men who travelled with him, such as Baptiste Bruneau and Baptiste Letendre, stayed in Alberta and the descendants of these vigorous and resourceful men are still around. The very first white men to come here had Aboriginal wives, so that the majority of people in the fur trade were what can roughly be called Métis (people of mixed race). These people were Louis' friends and colleagues and, later, his in-laws.

Entrepreneurs don't let danger or distance stop them. They invest the time and take the risks. The eighteenth-century fur trade was a particularly difficult business. To obtain the product, which was animal pelts, a company manager was totally dependent on decisions made by hundreds of individual trappers. An uncontrollable variable in the business was Nature which controlled fur animal populations. The trappers, too, had problems and challenges. In order to snare the fur-bearing creatures, families had to live near the bush where they could repeatedly visit long trap lines in the winter. The tedious job of preparing the skins followed. Then the pelts had to be packed to a trading post. Additionally, the time taken trapping furs and transporting them to a trader gave a man less time to hunt and fish on behalf of his family. Louis took on this challenge.

Getting the furs to market over thousands of miles of perilous waterways during the short summer required many skilled navigators, courageous men and large numbers of elegant and well-designed canoes. The furs were then shipped overseas. A great quantity of trade goods chosen to appeal to the largely Aboriginal trappers had to be sent from Europe by ship and transported to the far-flung trading posts and forts. The companies had to man forts all year round and provide employees with the necessities of life.

Obtaining enough food for all these men—many of whom had families to keep—was a persistant problem. For example, in 1810, new White Earth House on the North Saskatchewan River had a population of as many as 72 men, women, and children in houses and tents.[17] According to Parker, a man's daily allowance at Fort Chipewyan in the 1830s was eight pounds, (about sixteen fish.) Thus to feed everyone at a post would require taking hundreds of fish each day. To maintain the stores of food required freezing or drying, then they were stored in sheds or ice cellars.[71] When furs were scarce in one place, new posts had to be built where there was good trapping and adequate food sources. As the trappers became fussier and harder to please, more attractive and more numerous kinds of trade goods had to be obtained and distributed.

Trade goods came from Europe to Quebec, thence to Montreal and then by a very bad road for the short distance to Lachine. Louis would have left from this point in early May. He probably went up the Ottawa River which had a series of rapids that were the sites of many accidents. To run white water required all his strength and skill. The boats could also be brought through by hauling them with lines from the shore. If necessary, a portage was made, which meant that the goods and boats would be unloaded and carried around the site of the rapid. After the Ottawa River came Lake Nipissing. Then they went by French River to Georgian Bay, along the north shore into Lake Huron and to Sault Ste. Marie. When Louis arrived at Grand Portage which was, for a while, the distribution centre, annual exchanges of goods and furs took place and men were re-contracted. Other routes required that everything be conveyed overland to Lake Erie and then be moved west. Mail was carried by sledges and snowshoes, couriers leaving the North in November, to reach Sault Ste. Marie in March. There was also a summer express. The return trip for the boats was in September.

Louis paddled a craft known as the 'north' canoe that was about 25 feet in length and four or five feet wide. These were light-weight vessels made of thin sheets of birch bark sewn with strips of spruce roots, and the seams sealed with spruce gum. Each canoe was manned by eight to ten men. Louis had to supply his own carefully-hewn paddles. His personal baggage and more than sixty packages of goods might include six hundredweight of biscuit, two hundredweight of pork and three bushels of peas. What a diet! The men also brought an axe, a towing line, a kettle and some kind of sponge for bailing. Bark, gum and spruce roots were brought along for repairing the canoes. Louis had to be most careful in handling the trade goods. These were packed in casks, bags, crates, cans, baskets and bales which were arranged on poles laid on the bottom of the canoe with oilcloths over top for protection. At least 20% of the goods carried were kegs of liquor. Some trade items, such as maple sugar, were acquired on the way. Larger canoes could carry five tons and were 36 feet long by six feet wide. They weighed 500 pounds and might have to be portaged (carried over land) in addition to the packs.

Men routinely carried two packs of ninety pounds each—a load of about eighty kilograms. According to Mackenzie, some men could manage as many as seven packs at a time for a distance of half a league (or about three kilometres).[49] Louis worked twenty hours a day for two to three weeks with a ten-minute rest every two hours to smoke a pipe.[20] Alexander Ross was referring to men like Louis when he said that the Iroquois were known to be the best canoemen, especially in the "dangerous runs and rapids that they stem or shoot with the utmost skill."[81]

Louis likely carried the most surprising trade goods in his canoe. In addition to practical items like guns, blankets, capots (overcoats), shirts, tobacco, traps, axes, saws and knives, there were oilcloths, sugar, brassware, thimbles, hoes, children's robes, caps, and looking glasses. They even had oatmeal, dogs, fish, spears, silver ornaments and chief's hats with feathers. By 1814, the goods included gartering, pistols, gloves, perfumery, silk stockings and even umbrellas, cheese and colours for painting. You could get mathematical instruments, gilt ware and lime juice by 1818. The Northwest Company traders made themselves popular by giving brandy to the people who came in to trade. They were, of course, much criticized for this by their rivals in the Hudson's Bay Company, who were also known to dispense the gift of a 'dram'. Both companies gave liberal credit to encourage loyalty.

In addition to his wages, Louis, as a Northwest Company employee, or *engagé*, was provided with an 'outfit': leggings, shirts, tobacco, knives and beads. He probably received some vermilion, which was a sort of

Boat running rapid Slave River

Plate 3. Running Slave River Rapids, n.d.
photo from W.J. Carter Ms, courtesy University of Alberta

red-coloured grease paint. Higher ranking employees, the 'proprietors' and clerks were entitled to gifts such as tea, coffee and chocolate as well.

Imagine what Louis' life as a voyageur was like. He had to be physically strong and remarkably tough. He took pleasure when he could: a smoke, a chance to fish or to hunt. He could enjoy the customary party when he arrived at a fur trade post. There might be a dance, a feast and lots to drink. If he was lucky, he had a girl waiting for him. Then, he faced the river again, the storms and cold, hunger, and heavy, heavy loads. In the winter, at the trading posts, there were not only extremes of cold and bad weather, but deprivation and boredom. When he wasn't working, there was little to do besides eat, sleep and play cards. Some men liked to wrestle. There could be friction between the bosses and working men. Some clerks and traders felt very superior to the lower ranks. James Mackenzie of the Northwest Company said that a Canadian is seldom pleased "quand il n'engraisse pas" [when he's not getting fat]. Some of Louis' colleagues were alleged to have engaged in trickery, stealing and just plain laziness. The voyageurs were very 'macho'. For instance, Mackenzie tells us that one man was looked down on because he helped gather and carry moss for his baby so that his wife would only have to carry the child.[67 iii]

Around 1804, Louis travelled between the Northwest Company posts in the prairies which were divided into the following regions, "Upper and Lower Red River, Athabasca, Forts des Prairies, Jasper House, and Fort Dauphin."[52] There were also Hudson's Bay Company Posts on the North Saskatchewan, Athabasca, and Peace Rivers. The men at the posts underwent a round of endless activity—repairing buildings, building boats, planting crops. There were continuous comings and goings of employees, native people and other visitors. For *engagés*, such as Louis, procuring food by hunting or fishing was an additional task. There was always a threat from drunken or hostile Indians and from rival traders. There were even killings, looting and burning in the battles between the fur trade companies. For example, a Northwest Company servant was murdered by an employee of the short-lived XY Company in Saskatchewan in 1802.[71]

By 1805, Louis' contract with the company had a year remaining.[67 ii] He had already achieved the rank of steersman working out of Fort

Augustus (which was not far from Edmonton) in the Saskatchewan District. This meant a promotion from the position of middleman, who does the paddling, to the job of the person responsible for steering the canoe from the stern. He must have been competent for his age because his colleague, Joseph Belcourt, was still a middleman after twelve years service. Louis had also accumulated a debt with this company. Employees were given goods whose value was then deducted from their salaries. In addition to goods, the Company made arrangements to transfer funds to relatives and to pay debts, including money owed for religious services. Indeed, Antoine Savard (Louis' son-in-law) once had some wages coming to him and the account book said the amount was transferred, presumably to the clergy, "for prayers".[67 i]

Was it Louis Callihoo who joined David Thompson in May of 1810 on the west side of the Rockies near the head of the Columbia River? An Iroquois, called Louis, was there for the summer to guide and hunt for Thompson's Northwest Company people. He was to be steersman of a canoe for a salary of 600 livres [pounds] and was given an outfit. He would also receive an additional bonus for each large animal obtained and also for furs.[89]

Louis Callihoo would have met many different kinds of people. There had already been a westward movement of Aboriginal people at least as early as the eighteenth century. Some Cree and Chipewyan Nations had crossed the continent almost as far as the mountains and the Cree even extended down into the Plains. Local people, such as the Beaver, had their home range reduced and some northern folk, the Sarcee, had moved into the plains. The Sekani lived by the Athabasca River and in the mountains near Jasper House; while the Kootenays retreated over the mountains. Alexander Henry, a Northwest Company manager, said that a band of Courtes Oreilles came from Michilimakinac (Sault Ste. Marie) to Lesser Slave Lake before the nineteenth century.[17] Eventually, Assiniboine peoples came north and west from below the border to settle in Alberta.

The most numerous of the Aboriginal tribes were the enterprising Cree. By the end of the century, other peoples had taken on much of the Cree culture in the manner of their dress, ornamentation and customs. Many Aboriginal people learned not only French and English but took to speaking Cree, even if it was not their native tongue. Father Lacombe remarked that even the Assiniboine or "Stony" at Lac Ste-Anne spoke Cree.[44] Louis certainly spoke French, in addition to Iroquois, as evidenced by his conversations with post managers, and he must have picked up Cree from his relatives and neighbours.

When they had served their time, many *engagés* went back East; in fact, you were in default of your contract with the Northwest Company and called a deserter if you weren't discharged in Montreal. However, a post manager had the authority to rehire people or extend their contracts or give new contracts in the field. Some of these fur trade servants would accumulate so much debt that they could be pressured into signing on again to work it off. Among the men who preferred to stay employed rather than striking out independently was Olivier Bellerose, who worked for the Hudson's Bay Company and lived with his family at Lesser Slave Lake and at Edmonton. He was a neighbour and a relative of Louis' (his wife was the sister of Louis' son's wife). Bellerose transported goods by dog team in winter and by canoe in summer to headquarters in Edmonton. Besides the regular salary, and rations for the whole family, a person could earn a retirement pension for himself or his widow this way.

As an alternative to signing on again or returning to Montreal, many voyageurs left company employment to become 'freemen'. They colonized Red River or remained on the great rivers to make their living independently by hunting and trapping. Louis, like many other Iroquois, engaged at Sault St. Louis, went to the region served by Jasper House when freed. D.W. Harmon, of the post at Fort Dunvegan, mentions Iroquois coming in to Fort Vermilion to trade in 1808.[34] Although there were reported to be over two hundred Iroquois in the West at the end of the eighteenth century, only a few families persisted in Alberta very far into the nineteenth. Amongst these were the Joachims, Wanyandis, Mondions, Karakontis, Gauchers, Grays, and, of course, some Callihoos. Some chose to go west over the mountains and fourteen were murdered in 1802 by some Gros Ventres on the Plains.[39] The rest probably went home.

In some places, the freemen were so successful that they eventually outnumbered the local Cree population.

Freeman

Louis was still working for the Northwest Company between 1812 and 1814, but now in the Athabasca region.[67 i] His friend, Ignace Wanyandi, who was on the same employee list as Louis in 1804,[53] was signed up with this company too. Fifty years later, their grandchildren would marry each other. After 1814, Louis was known as a 'freeman' which means that he was no longer on contract but was quite independent.

He may well have been the "Louis, an Iroquois Indian," who travelled with Ross Cox's party through an area which included Jasper Park's present location. Early in June 1817, Cox's men built a wooden raft in order to bring their supplies across the Rocky River, a tributary of the Athabasca. The horses had crossed over safely but when four men, including Louis, tried to cross on the raft, they were carried into the rapids instead and went downstream with terrifying rapidity from one cascade to another for two miles. Then the raft started to break up from the pounding it was getting on the rocks! Just when there seemed no hope of escape from going over a cataract, the raft slowed in a counter current above the falls. Louis and the other men were able to jump overboard into shallow water and were even able to grab and save the raft with all their things. They ended up at the old Rocky Mountain House post manned by Jasper Hawse.[18] Louis probably remained here and didn't go on with the others to Winnipeg because he is not mentioned again in Cox's journal.

Family Man and Provider

J. G. MacGregor, the historian, says that Louis Callihoo was at Jasper House in 1811 and that he had been there since 1805.[47] Here was where Louis probably met Marie Katis, a girl of the Sekani tribe, and one of the two women with whom he spent the rest of his life. Father Lacombe gave the sacrement of Christian marriage to Louis and Marie Katis on 16 October, 1853 at Jasper.[68 xiv] On the occasion of her baptism, a few days before their wedding the priest writes that she was sixty years old. Louis' oldest well-documented child was Thomas, who was born around 1815. There might well have been older sons and daughters who did not get baptized and thus were simply not recorded some thirty-five years later. One such son was known as Louis Dekara. This man's children, Louis and Nancy, claimed in 'half-breed' scrip applications in 1900 that their grandparents were Louis Karaconti and Marie Sekani.[23 xxi] Louis Karakonti called Dekara was baptised and married Marguerite Cardinal in 1853 at Jasper on the same day as his parents were married.[68 xiv]

Marie Katis may have travelled with Louis when they were both young but she probably made her home and raised her children in the Smoky River Valley throughout much of her life with him. In 1825, Louis had a camp near the forks of the Smoky River.[38 iv] Other Iroquois freemen are also reported to have lived near the Smoky River.[41] They had good reasons. Some Iroquois told Dr. Hector, a naturalist who accompanied the Palliser Expedition, that "it is the finest land in the country." There are extensive prairies along the river valley and good pasture in all seasons. They said that there were herds of bison and elk. Wild fruit was always plentiful and because of this there were numbers of black bear and grizzlies. They also told him that the Iroquois had even grown potatoes, turnips and barley there.[70] We must suppose that the Hudson's Bay Company sold the precious seed in the mid-eighteen hundreds.

Not very far from Fort Augustus was another trading post called White Earth House. Henry reported that Patenaude, a freeman, was at White Earth House with his family in 1810.[17] He had a Cree wife, Françoise, and a few children. This Patenaude, maybe called Michel, worked for the Northwest Company in 1804 in a supervisory position as a "voyageur contre maitre" or foreman, in the Upper Red River region.[17] In 1805, he

Scrip is a term used to describe a kind of certificate rather like a cheque. It entitles the owner, and in some cases the bearer, to the amount on its face, subject to regulations set by the producer of the scrip. The Department of the Interior issued so called "half-breed" scrip that designated numbers of acres or amounts of money. However, in either case, it was redeemable only for land. When scrip was first devised, an acre of land was deemed to be worth one dollar. The purpose of scrip was to provide the land required in order that the Métis people could make a living by agriculture. It recognized Aboriginal entitlement but precluded any further claim. The Department administered and arbitrated each individual's claim to be a half-breed. Certain Crown lands were set aside for scrip purposes although it appears that some people were able to obtain other Crown property on request. As it turned out, the lands available were often too far away or otherwise not desirable, and so people commonly did not wish to use their particular allotment. Many Métis people, therefore, sold their scrip to speculators. In 1885, they were paid between $40 and $80 for $160 scrip, and for $240 scrip about $125.

was a foreman in the same region.[67 ii] Patenaude had died by 1821, when two of his sons were known to the people at the Hudson's Bay Company Fort at Lesser Slave Lake. Louis Callihoo met the Patenaude family at some point and took up with two of the daughters. He had at least two children with Josephte Patenaude and seven with Marie Patenaude.[68 xiii] It appears that these last two families made their home at Lesser Slave Lake, for the most part. Hudson's Bay Company records show that Louis spent his time in both the Smoky River area and at Lesser Slave Lake.

Louis made a good living hunting, trapping and freighting and so was able to look after all his wives and children. Some people were engaged specifically to hunt furs, a scheme that was so effective that the company could afford to offer these workers half price on goods they needed. This practice continued until the middle of the nineteenth century. The Iroquois had the reputation of being the most aggressive fur hunters of all. Their habitual use of steel traps contributed to their success.[64] In his 1827 journal for Jasper House, Michael Klyne said that he wouldn't give the Assiniboine trading credit, because it is all reserved for the Iroquois freemen who bring in the furs and whom, he hopes, won't go away.[41] He was certainly including Louis in this group as he discusses his dealings with him in the same journals.

As late as the 1880s, the Beaver people at Fort Dunvegan resented the Iroquois Métis for their excellent trapping ability and diligence.[32] Iroquois freemen had a poor reputation for another reason, according to Colin Campbell of the Hudson's Bay Company at Fort Dunvegan. He said of the Fort Assiniboine freemen, "These rascally Iroquois fill the Indian's [sic] heads with many things very detrimental to the Company's interest." The Iroquois freemen used to shift their custom from fort to fort in order to obtain better prices. Instead of admiring them for their cleverness, Company traders considered them "spoiled".

Louis also traded at Lesser Slave Lake from 1816 on[38 iv] and at Fort Dunvegan.[65] Between 1821 and 1825, Lesser Slave Lake fur returns included grizzly and black bears, cats, elk, goats, fisher, wolf and otter,

---

A number of reports repeat the story that Patenaude was a failed Hudson's Bay Company Factor from Fort Carlton. I have found no original record of this. There appears to be no Patenaude in the list of opposition traders in Johnson, 1967.[39]

in addition to beaver. Some of these were traded by Louis. There was a market for other things, too. On October 19, 1821, Louis is said to have twenty bags of pemmican with which to pay his debts. In the spring of 1825, he was paid the equivalent of 107 MB in prime furs. This term, MB, or "made beaver" was a standard value, and was referred to as amounts of currency are used elsewhere. Louis brought beaver pelts, other furs and possibly castorium (valuable material from a beaver's oil glands, used in making perfume) to Fort Edmonton, too.

Was there a risk to Louis and his families when violence broke out between the rival companies? Were the Callihoos at Lesser Slave Lake during the "little war", a battle between the Hudson's Bay Company and the Northwest Company? During this episode, it is said that four or five men were killed and buried on an island that came to be known as "Dead Man's Island".[5] Alexander Stewart of the Northwest Company led his men in an attack on a Hudson's Bay Company Post around 1819. He seized and partly destroyed the post and took the managers prisoner.[37 iii] Clients made trouble as well. Some Aboriginal people occasionally stole horses or engaged in violent acts against traders or against their neighbours because of fur trade jealousies. The two major companies finally amalgamated in 1821. After this, some of the main competition came from American interests.

Louis may have helped create some of the trouble, himself. In August 1819, when he sold a canoe to the Hudson's Bay Company post manager at Lesser Slave Lake, the Northwest Company men just next door claimed it was theirs! What brought about this misunderstanding? Had Louis bought the canoe or received it in payment for services, and this was just normal hostility between the companies, or had he or his friends appropriated it?

Perhaps Louis had benefited from the competition between the rival companies. The aggressive competition for furs between the Aboriginal

---

Louis' great-granddaughter, Beatrice, says that her grandfather described something of two wives and their families living in the same home. She heard that there was a low partition in the main room. Possibly this describes a house where her grandfather Michel grew up with his mother and her sister and their children.

trappers and newcomers and amongst rival companies caused the companies to change the location of posts rather frequently in order to entice trappers. They were built at various locations at Lesser Slave Lake, as well as on the Peace River, and there were very important supply posts on the North Saskatchewan River. Both companies maintained forts in the vicinity of what is now Edmonton.

This policy would certainly have influenced Louis' decisions. For example, in 1823, Connelly, of the post at Lesser Slave Lake, recommended, and Governor Simpson agreed, that a post in the Smoky River area be reoccupied for the greater convenience of freemen and Iroquois who might otherwise be tempted to cross the mountains to hunt, Rocky Mountain House being too remote for them.[38 iv] On the other hand, Jasper House was on the Athabasca River in 1824, and was moved eighty to a hundred miles north on the Smoky River to try to keep freemen from trading at Lesser Slave Lake. By 1857, after Louis' time, the Jasper House post was said to be poorly attended by the descendants of "Iroquois half-breeds". This may have been because many people had moved to Lac Ste-Anne, including many of Louis' sons and daughters.

Louis, the Man

We know little of Louis' habits or clothes, but we know about some of his contemporaries. A compatriot of his, François Xavier Tarihonque, was a very natty dresser. In 1825, François outfitted himself at Lesser Slave Lake with cambray (a kind of fine white linen) trousers, striped cotton shirts and a blue capot made of stroud (a kind of blanket cloth). He bought silk and cotton handkerchiefs. François Xavier topped all this off with a woolen hat for which he bought a cover and "fox tail feathers", a cock feather and four tassels in two colours! He also bought a pair of strong shoes. Having all this finery, it is not surprising that he then got three bars of soap, some thread and some needles. François Xavier also obtained a large striped blanket, four clay pipes and some tobacco.

Louis may have dressed like that in his youth but when he was in his forties (1822), he bought just plain cord trousers which he wore with a red sash. He also got a woolen hat but decorated it with only a plain silk cover.[38 vi]

Louis accumulated a credit balance with the Hudson's Bay Company of £28/10/– in 1828. At this time, he is called a "colonist" in the account book.[38 iv] It's a good thing that he is successful for by now he has at least eight children to support.

An anecdote tells us something of his character and his affection for horses. Michel Klyne was post manager at Jasper House and was well acquainted with Louis. When, on June 24, 1829, Klyne found himself short of horses for an imminent journey, he exchanged his four mares for four of Louis' horses for the season. Klyne remarked that he knew that Louis would take good care of them.[41]

Louis Callihoo signed no more long-term work contracts after about 1815, but he took on odd jobs for the Hudson's Bay Company, such as hauling goods to the Lesser Slave Lake post in 1819.[66] He was also there in 1820, working on a building before he left on November 30 to accompany another man on a trip. In 1821, he was employed by the Lesser Slave Lake post to bring back furs from the spring hunt in the Rocky Mountains.[38 ivv] He worked over the next two decades at various jobs, even getting birch bark and arranging it into packs in November of 1835.[2]

To Louis, the rivers and trails of west central Alberta must have been as familiar as streets in their home towns are to taxi drivers. He travelled by boat, on horseback and no doubt by dog team, too. Each year, throughout the 1820s, Louis visited the Lesser Slave Lake post in the winter and again in the spring.[38 iv] He travelled with his in-laws, the Patenaude brothers, with "old" Hamelin, Antoine Gouin, Charles Gladu and Chief Factor Rowand's son, Antoine, and often brought a good hunt of furs and sometimes some pemmican. Louis was a familiar visitor at various western posts. He went to Fort Edmonton in the spring of 1828, bringing the news and business gossip from Fort Assiniboine. He is mentioned in the Fort Edmonton journal for that year, being one of the freemen seen by Mr. Harriott and from whom he "got a tolerable hunt in martens." Louis obtained some metal traps and ironworks, and headed back to Fort Assiniboine with "Old Delorme"[38 i] (who was probably his daughter's father-in-law). Did they travel on the Athabasca River and then use horses on the nasty muskeg of the Assiniboine Trail, or did they go the long way round on the rivers? In November of that year Louis was encamped at Lesser Slave Lake.[38 ii]

Louis and his teen-aged son, Thomas, could have been the Iroquois who came down to Edmonton from the Beaver River in January of 1833 as mentioned in the Fort Edmonton journals.[38 i] It was dangerous to travel in these years, especially on the edge of the Plains. Horse stealing was very common. During the earlier period of intense rivalry between the fur companies, a person could have been caught in a deadly battle during an attack on a fort.

Louis Callihoo is regularly on the Hudson's Bay Company books in the 1830s. He no doubt continued to hunt furs. He also did some serious fishing, as evidenced by the fact that he bought net thread in 1840.[38 vi] On the same occasion, he got some shirts, a belt and as much as 35 yards of material, including striped and printed cotton, stroud in different colours, and tartan, probably wool. In addition, he got some luxuries: two pairs of gilt earrings and some crushed sugar. This all cost £12/16/3. His trapping luck must have held because in the following year he bought nearly £11 worth of goods, including a number of blankets of different weights, 23 more yards of material, more shirts, some tinned iron table spoons, soap, needles, thread, some tea, black pepper and more sugar. He also got some cod line and a couple of knives.

From 1841 to 1845, Louis was hired each year to carry freight on the Saskatchewan, to York Factory and Norway House, and between Lesser Slave Lake and Edmonton.[38 iv] He would make about £4 for the whole trip at a time when a horse was worth about £2. While working for the company he would be provided with rations of pemmican, biscuit, flour and some pork. Louis sold the company grease and butter in the winter and earned a little money making covers and cords for bales of furs. He had a debt as high as £82 at the beginning of 1842 but paid much of it off with furs. On such trips to York Factory in the 1840s accompanied by his young son, Michel, he bought two common and two fine shirts with blue and white stripes, a broad scarlet belt, some capots to keep warm, and to top it all off two "Highland bonnet caps". He also bought army lace garters, eight cotton handkerchiefs, a spotted muslin handkerchief, worsted and silk handkerchiefs, yards goods in the form of striped blue cotton, plain blue cotton, scarlet cloth, some blue strouds, duffle, ferrets (narrow bands of cloth) and needles, with plain and coloured thread and silk. He also bought decorations in the form of coloured ribbon and white enamel beads. For his womenfolk he got horn combs and an ivory comb. The other things on his list of purchases were blankets, tea, sugar, salt, clay pipes, scissors, scalping knives, cod line, twine, tobacco and a tobacco box.

Louis' children with Marie and Josephte Patenaude are referred to in the chapter about their brother, Michel Callihoo. By 1830, Josephte Patenaude appears to have moved and she ended up marrying André Papin at Fort Carlton in 1842.[68 xiv] She had at least four more children with him.

Louis' children with Marie Katis are more difficult to trace. One was Louis Dekara/Karaconti, who married a Marguerite Cardinal, a descendent of Joseph Cardinal and Joseph Frobisher (the former a French-Canadian, the latter a Métis). Their daughter, Suzanne, Jasper Post Manager Henry Moberley's wife, is buried in what is now Jasper Park. This Louis Dekara known as "Tekarra" by Dr. Hector of the Palliser expedition was hired as a guide in 1859. He was to take Hector and Moberley to the source of the Athabasca River and thence to Lac Ste-Anne. Hector remarked on Louis' unusual stamina (with an injured foot) and his hunting prowess. Louis Dekara was also the man who once offered to trade one of his tall and strong daughters for a horse. Cheadle, a private adventurer, hired an "Old Louis l'Iroquois" to guide

---

Louis' (1782–1854) children include:

with Marie Katis (1793–?): Louis *dit* Dekara (?–?) married Marguerite Cardinal; Thomas (1815–?) married Suzanne Desjarlais then Louise, then Angélique Finlay; Therèse (1816–1878) married François Berland; Marie Anne (1822–?) married Simon Wanatch; Suzanne (1824–?) married Joseph Gaucher; Marie (1826–1877) married Louis Campbell *dit* Pelletier; Ignace (1829–1867) married Marguerite Beaudry; Michel (1831–?);

with Josephte Patenaude (1812–?): Josephte (1822–1850) married Charles Beauregard; Suzanne (1827–1865) married Joseph Gray;

with Marie Patenaude (1803–1854): Michel (1824–1911) married Marie Savard then Philomène Collin; Thomas (1830–1874) married Marguerite Collin then Marie Finlay; Jean Baptiste (1832–1910) married Angélique Bruneau; Cécile (1834–?) married Jean Baptiste Belcourt then Edward Berland Valade; Angélique (1838–1908) married Louis Loyer; Marguerite (1841–1866) married Pierre Delorme; Louis (1845–1865).

his party through the mountains in 1863. He has also been called Louis "Carpontier". This was very likely the same Louis Dekara who was last seen by Cheadle "crooning" to the horse he was given in payment.[16] Was fondness for horses a family trait?

Louis' son, Thomas Kwarakwante, was mentioned when he traded as a freeman with the Hudson's Bay Company. Church records tell us that Therèse Kwarakwante married François Berland (whose brother later married her half-sister Cécile Callihoo.) Their children seemed to have stayed in the mountain area. Two or three other daughters married Iroquois freemen. Ignace married Marguerite Beaudry and lived at Lac Ste-Anne where he is believed by recent family members to have been murdered by a jealous husband.

Louis' relatives and connections could be found in many places. A Patenaude, who may be Louis' brother-in-law, is mentioned in Fort Edmonton journals, as are a number of other in-laws. Some were freemen and others were employed by the Hudson's Bay Company such as Charles Beauregard, a French-Canadian who married Louis' daughter, Josephte. Joseph Belcourt worked at Lesser Slave Lake in the 1820s, as did Louis Loyer, Jacques L'Hirondelle, and Antoine Savard. With the exception of Josephte, all Louis' children married Métis people with an Ojibway, Cree, Sekani or Iroquois background. They did not tend to marry into the First Nations families who were indigenous to the country. Louis' children spoke Cree, knew how to speak French and may have had a little Iroquois. At least one, Michel, also spoke English.

By 1838, Louis had at least fifteen children. He was listed in the Native census of Lesser Slave Lake.[38 iv] Robert Rundle, the Wesleyan missionary, said that there were two freemen's houses at Shaw's Point where Louis lived in 1842. This was nine miles from the Company post along the north shore of the lake. It was from here, on April 6, 1842, that Louis sent for Mr. Rundle, the only Christian cleric available, to attend to him when he "supposed himself to be near death," to quote the Reverend. Rundle rushed off at once in a dog cariole (a kind of sleigh with sides), arrived at Louis' place late in the evening and spent the night, not returning to the fort until noon the following day. He went back to Louis' on the ninth and slept in the sick man's room where there were already twenty people. No wonder he remarked on a bad smell. He held religious services in Louis' room on April tenth and made it back to the fort early next day. On his way out, on the third of May he spent one more night at Shaw's Point and says that he "saw poor Louis perhaps for the last time." In 1844, Rundle visited the place again and found the houses on the Point deserted but saw Louis' wife, Marie Patenaude, his son, Michel and a son-in-law, Joseph Gray, at the fort settlement.[76] It seems that "poor Louis" didn't turn out to be all that ill, but lived to know that his children were baptized in the Roman Catholic faith. Robert Rundle returned to Lesser Slave Lake two years later and sheltered in one of these houses at Shaw's Point.

Louis had returned to the mountains as usual. For some reason he and as many as 36 other people were gathered on the banks of what is probably the Athabasca River, near Jasper, in 1846. Father de Smet met them there and claimed that they were members of Louis' family. It was he who originally referred to Louis as the "Traveller of the Sun". Louis was quoted by this Jesuit priest as saying, "How glad I am to have come here, for I have not seen a priest for many years. Today I behold a priest, as I did in my own country—my heart rejoices—wherever you go I shall follow you with my children—all will have happiness to receive baptism. Therefore my heart rejoices and is happy." Father de Smet wrote, "the little Iroquois camp immediately set out to follow me to Fort Jasper. Most of them know their prayers in Iroquois. I remained fifteen days at the Fort, instructing them in the duties of religion—after Mass, on Sunday, all were regenerated in the waters of baptism, and seven marriages renewed and blessed."[79]

What a joyous Easter Sunday it must have been! Seven of Louis' children with Marie Katis as well as seven grandchildren were baptized on this occasion. Louis "Bonhomme" Loyer and François Berland each served as godfathers to some of them. The other people who received the sacraments of the Church on this day included some members of Ignace Kwarakwonte's family, and Louis acted as their godfather. Louis also extended his Christian responsibilities as godfather to the children of Augustin Delorme and to some orphan children of Baptiste Gaucher. Two of Louis' children, Thomas and Therèse, were married to their spouses by the visiting Father. In addition, Colin Fraser and his family,

Louis' in-laws, two Aboriginal children and a few other unrelated Métis were baptized.[79]

The members of Louis' other family also partook of the sacraments of the Church. Josephte Patenaude and her children with Louis were baptized in 1842, most likely at Fort Carlton by Father Thibeault. Marie Patenaude and her children were baptized at Lesser Slave Lake by Father Bourassa in 1845 and 1846.[68 xiv]

Louis' name remained from year to year on the list of freemen in the financial records kept by the Hudson's Bay Company at York Factory. Sometimes they owed him money, sometimes he was in debt to them. In 1851, he was in the red by £1/12/6. After 1852, the balance remained the same until 1858, when his name is gone. The name reappears in the book for the year 1862 but a line is drawn through it.[38 vi]

The priest who married Louis' son, Jean Baptiste Callihoo, to Angélique Bruneau on November 30, 1854 wrote in the register that both parents, Marie Patenaude and Louis Callihoo, were deceased. The same information was entered when their daughter Marguerite married Pierre Delorme in 1856.[68 xiv] The Sun Traveller was gone, aged nearly 72 years, leaving behind at least 105 grandchildren and thousands of living descendants to remember him. One notable descendant was his son, Michel, and his story follows.

A descendent of Louis l'Iroquois (Sid Karakonti) said that his grave is in the Wilmore Wilderness. There is a grave site and cross there, known as the 'small grave', where some people say Louis is buried.

Plate 4. Little Grave Flats, Willmore Wilderness Park
courtesy Jack Deenik

MICHEL CALLIHOO

This is the story of a great man: a fur trade employee, a freeman, a chief. His story also reflects the experiences of many Native people in Alberta.

Michel Callihoo came into the world around 1824. His mother was Marie Patenaude, a daughter of a Northwest Company employee and his Cree wife, Françoise. As described previously, Michel's father, Louis Callihoo, was a well-known Iroquois freeman who made his living hunting and trapping in the vast and beautiful country between the Athabasca and Smoky Rivers. Marie, her younger sister, Josephte, and their children probably made their home at Lesser Slave Lake while Michel was growing up.

If we try to picture Michel's childhood, we see him being bossed by his older half-sister and playing with his younger brothers. His father travelled a lot but was at home for a while in the winter and spring when Michel was very young. For instance, in 1826, Louis was at Lesser Slave Lake for Christmas. Perhaps the whole family enjoyed the New Year's dance held at the fort that year.[38 iv] He must have gone hunting and trapping with his dad and no doubt learned from him how to build and repair boats and manage horses. He accompanied his father on at least one freighting trip to York Factory. Michel told his son Solomon that he learned to read the weather and understand the behaviour of rivers and lakes from his own father. Michel must have been competent and confident because, when he was still in his teens, he already had work with the Hudson's Bay Company. According to his nephew's wife, Victoria Callihoo, Michel was over six-feet tall, fair-skinned and reported by others to have been good-looking.[35]

When the Callihoo children were still young, the Hudson's Bay Company had a vaccination program at their woodland forts, including

Lesser Slave Lake, to prevent the spread of smallpox during the epidemic of 1837–1838.[74] We don't know if any Callihoo children were vaccinated, nor if any became infected; however, none of Michel's brothers and sisters died during another epidemic of this deadly disease in 1870.

When he was about twenty, Michel married sixteen-year-old Marie Savard, whose father, Antoine Savard, had been a voyageur from French Canada employed in the 1820s at Lesser Slave Lake. Her mother, Marie Anne Lavallée, was widowed when Marie was only four and supported her family by selling moose hides and other things to the Hudson's Bay Company. Marie's sister, Suzette, married Olivier Bellerose, a Hudson's Bay Company employee, and they, too, lived at Lesser Slave Lake. Her brothers, Alexander and Antoine, were also employed by the Company. In later years the two increased their family ties because some of the Savard nieces and nephews married Callihoo nieces and nephews. Marie and Michel took the opportunity on 20 April, 1846, to be baptized and joined in marriage by the Roman Catholic priest, Father Bourassa, at Lesser Slave Lake, right under the nose of the opposition, a Methodist minister who was visiting at the time.[68 xiv] Michel's father had taught his children that a man wearing a large cross on his chest was the kind of Christian they should choose to give them the sacraments. Michel's godfather was the priest himself.

Michel was engaged by the Hudson's Bay Company in the 1840s. It is reported by family members that his work took him out on the rivers from Athabasca to Fort Garry. As early as 1842, Michel was paid £6/0/2 as a "trip man"—more money than any one of the other eleven men on the list! He reminds us of his father, Louis.

Michel was at Lesser Slave Lake in May 1846, when he had to take the Welsleyan missionary, Robert Rundle, to Fort Assiniboine. He was staying with his mother, and the Reverend was under the impression that she was a widow, but in reality her partner was at Jasper with his other family at the time. Michel gave Rundle breakfast and fed his dog team some fish

---

The family of Antoine Savard (1792–1832) and Marie Anne Lavallée (1795–1872): Suzette (1826–1891) married Olivier Bellerose; Antoine (1827–1917) married Marguerite Bisson; Marie (1828–1869) married Michel Callihoo; Angélique (?–?) married Alexander Fisher; Alexander (1832–?) married Therèse Bisson; Joseph (?–?).

as well. They started out on the trip by sledge and then had to switch to canoes. Mr. Rundle conducted prayer services in Michel's tent whenever they stopped.[76] Was this when Michel first learned some English?

In 1847, Michel had his first long-term contract as a middleman in the Hudson's Bay Company, making a yearly wage of £17 with £7 in gratuities for acting as steersman. He achieved a promotion two years later to steersman for £25 per year.[38 vi] Michel had a credit of nearly £7 at this time even though he already had four children! (The Company would let its employees have the goods they wanted, and deducted their value from salaries.) A Company journal mentions that Michel was with his family in the spring of 1849 when he did some freighting with horses from Fort Assiniboine to Edmonton. This is probably when he moved his family from Lesser Slave Lake to Fort Edmonton.

Fort Edmonton was an essential centre for providing provisions and other supplies to the Hudson's Bay Company posts in the hinterlands. It is situated in an area known to ecologists as "Parkland". Here stretches of forest are interspersed with grasslands. There is plenty of water and a comparatively moderate climate. This fertile region attracted long- and short-term settlers because bison were never far away and the woods abounded with other game. There was even adequate grazing for horses. You could also grow potatoes and a few vegetables. The river, itself, with its tributaries, was an excellent thoroughfare for the transport of furs, goods and people.

Lifestyle

In the days of the western fur trade people rarely settled down in one place for long. Some people built homes around the posts but often had to move to make a better living. The settlements of Lac Ste-Anne and St. Albert, not far to the northwest of Fort Edmonton, were established by missionaries. Their plan was for stable communities to develop. Almost all the first citizens of the mission towns were Métis, that is, the freemen of the fur trade era, and incidentally, relatives of Michel Callihoo. Before the bison were gone and the fur-bearing animals depleted, these people developed an increasingly comfortable lifestyle depending mainly on trading furs for goods and on hunting bison for food. The Hudson's Bay

Company Journal of 1855 tells us that freemen from Lac Ste-Anne traded three hundred marten at one time. The notes say that in the following year they even increased the numbers of animals caught. Fur animals provided some of the income for people in this region at least until the turn of the century, even though the numbers of many species declined markedly, partly because of the continual harvest.

The Mission at Lac Ste-Anne was founded in 1843 by Father Thibeault, a member of the Order of Marie Immaculate. It is situated not far to the north and west of Edmonton in a forested area. Although some of the Iroquois freemen are said to have moved to Lac Ste-Anne in 1856, Father Lacombe still made the eleven-day journey out west on horseback to administer the sacraments to the rest of the people who lived in colonies near Jasper. He points out that it was a good thing that the Jasper Iroquois gave him six horses, as some Blackfoot had stolen the ones at Lac Ste-Anne.[44] As they had stolen from the Hudson's Bay Company years before, in 1833, it seems they were still up to their old tricks.[38i]

A new mission was built by the Oblates in 1861 and called St. Albert after its first priest, Father Albert Lacombe. It is situated on the Sturgeon River just north of Edmonton and was chosen for the fertile soil, which they hoped would support farming. Twenty-one Métis families moved there from Lac Ste-Anne.

Bison were a vital part of the economy of these people. They provided the essential and preferred source of food in addition to leather, sinew, raw hide cord, robes and some utensils. When she was only thirteen, in 1874, Victoria Belcourt accompanied her mother and brother bison hunting. Her father stayed home.

She described the hunt seventy-six years later:[11] after the people of Lac Ste-Anne planted their vegetable gardens each spring and by the time the poplar leaves were out they would trundle off in their carts to St. Albert. There the carts were loaded with things they needed for the plains, including tent poles, firewood, birch bark and flint. They picked up friends and relatives, then continued on to Edmonton where more people joined the group. A priest usually accompanied his flock. At some point, the leading men met and chose a leader for the hunt from amongst themselves. He flew a flag over his cart to identify his authority. The party traversed the

North Saskatchewan River, carts, children, horses, oxen and all their baggage until they came to where the Provincial Legislature now stands. That crossing must have been quite a sight! Some one hundred people then headed south to set up camps in the region north of Red Deer where the last remaining herds of bison still roamed. The carts were placed in a circle as a kind of defensive barrier, because the Aboriginal People of the plains very much resented the incursion of the Métis into their territories. The horses also needed to be guarded at night. Ironically, the best horses were obtained by barter from the Blackfoot.

The hunting method was to run the bison down on horseback and shoot them. Some people had muzzle-loaders with caps, others had single-barreled flintlocks. The animals were then butchered and the meat hung up to dry. It was later dumped onto a buffalo hide and pounded to a pulp by four men. Melted grease and berries were added to improve the flavour and food value. In some places, birch trees were tapped to get the sap to run out. It was made into sugar and added. This concentrated dried mixture, called 'pemmican', was a very important staple in the diet of people in the West. Some people obtained enough meat at this time for the winter. Others returned to the hunt in the fall after the hay was in, while the 'hivernants' [winterers] spent the winter at Buffalo Lake where bison had been hunted for thousands of years.

The season was too short to ripen most of the available varieties of wheat, but barley, potatoes and root vegetables could be grown. The barley had to be hulled by pounding and then it could be eaten in soup, cooked in a frying pan or dried and then roasted black and stewed, to be drunk like coffee. In 1868 at Lac Ste-Anne, 700 barrels of potatoes, 200 of cabbage, carrots and onions were grown in addition to some wheat and barley. Fancy extras such as tea and sugar came from the Hudson's Bay Company store. Moose, deer and the occasional bear were much enjoyed for dinner, and their skins provided material for trousers, jackets, moccasins and mittens. Wild ducks and geese were also hunted and could be cooked whole on an open fire.

Everyone picked strawberries, raspberries, saskatoons and cranberries in the summer. Berries could be sun-dried and kept in a bag or used as an ingredient of pemmican. If you had glass containers you could make various preserves including a kind called "scratch". This delicious jam is prepared with whole chokecherries. The stones are not removed, but bashed into tiny pieces and cooked with the fruit for added flavour. Birch and Poplar sap were used for their sugar content.

Nowadays, it takes a real effort of imagination to picture how hard people had to work to keep food on the table, to keep warm and to keep clean. Teepees made of bark were sometimes used as temporary dwellings. Birch bark was best if aged for up to a year in a hole in the ground before it was used. Victoria Callihoo described the sort of house that Michel Callihoo would have built.[10] It was constructed of hewn logs which were also chinked and plastered with clay. They also made hewn log floors. To prepare the logs, men used large broadaxes and eight-foot-long, two-handled saws. To employ such a whip saw, platforms were built ten feet high and a log would be hoisted up. There was a man on top and another on the ground. They pulled the saw up and down; the down stroke did the cutting. Roof rafters were made of poles about three feet apart and on a quarter pitch angle. These were covered with spruce bark shingles laid with the shiny inner side underneath, and finally, pinned down with long poles set crosswise.

A common alternative to this kind of roof was one made of grass sods laid over the rafters. These provided good insulation. Windows were covered in parchment made of fawn skin with the hair removed. When the wet hide was nailed to the window, it would dry very taut and be stretched thin enough to let some light in. Open fireplaces were built kitty-corner to the door and constructed of mud and hay; and then whitewashed with white clay. The chimney projected well above the roof and the floor was plastered near the fireplace as a precaution against fire. They inserted iron bars (sometimes old gun barrels) in order to hang the various copper and iron kettles they obtained from the Hudson's Bay Company. Michel Callihoo bought such a copper kettle in 1851 for £0/16/11. There was no furniture but for a cupboard put together with wooden pegs because nails were scarce. At meal times, food was kept off the floor with a canvas cloth.

In time, as cattle became available, oxen assisted with the heavy farm work. Victoria said they hitched up one animal at a time, as they had only single harness. Ten-inch ploughs were used and then followed with a wooden harrow. They seeded by hand. Most people also kept horses.

To feed the livestock, they cut wild hay with Armstrong scythes. They gathered it with all-wood forks and then it was cocked or stooked. Two poles were pushed under the stooks by two men who lifted them and moved them to a stack. Sometimes, the hay was stacked onto small racks which had runners so that the oxen could haul them home in winter. By the 1870s, people also kept hogs and poultry.

Bedding was made with wild bird feathers stuffed into Hudson's Bay Company blankets and was rolled up each morning to make room. Some people had buffalo robes to sleep on while some made blankets out of strips of rabbit skin.

People made all kinds of other things for themselves, including soap ('la potash') made of ashes and grease. Brooms could be devised of coarse grasses or willow branches. Light was produced by burning animal grease with a twist of cloth or string for a wick. Before matches were available, a spark was made with flint and steel. They fabricated fish nets with store-bought string. Numerous tools were manufactured from salvaged metal. Some useful objects, such as kegs made by their employees, were sold by the Hudson's Bay Company.

Even though they could now purchase metal pots, people still knew how to make containers out of birch bark, sewing them with fine roots and sealing the seams with spruce gum. After they acquired cows, they used milk pans made of bark in this way.[10]

There was little cash available for store-bought things like clothes and shoes. Actual currency was not used much in Alberta by Native people until after the treaties were signed and cash payments made by the government. Transactions were normally done by barter.

If you didn't like the goods or prices at the Hudson's Bay Company store, you had to travel over a thousand miles to Red River to shop. As quoted from the Edmonton House journals of 1855,[38i] "This morning we beheld with vexation five of the Lake St. Anns freemen with 21 horses crossing the River below the Fort on their way to Red River, carrying away with them 500 martens together with other valuable furs to be sold there." However, the journey to St. Boniface took up to eight weeks because each cumbersome cart was pulled by only one animal.

The small cart was commonly hitched up to a horse or ox to carry families, buffalo meat and goods, on trails and even over fields and through the bush. The classic 'Red River cart' was made entirely of wood and consisted of a box fastened to a crude axle with tapered ends. The two wheels were either discs or made of several curved pieces that were dove-tailed together to form a rim. Spokes joined this to a hub. Wooden dowels and bison-hide strips held the pieces together. Two twelve-foot poles lashed to the box served as frame and shafts. Sometimes a strip of hide was placed over the wheel rims to soften the ride.[1] Tallow was applied as a lubricant in an attempt to quiet these noisy vehicles. With a cart like this, an ox could pull half a ton and make fifteen miles in a day. The carts were easy to convert to rafts in order to cross rivers.

Red River carts were once a common sight on the Lac Ste-Anne Trail which was first cut by Father Thibeault in 1844 in order to get to and from his new Mission. It came off the Fort Assiniboine Trail and led to Edmonton. In addition, people kept dogs which they hitched to a toboggan or cariole for winter travel. To travel more quickly using the waterways, men built birch bark canoes or dug-out boats constructed of large trees. To make a dug-out they simply hewed the outside to shape and scooped out the inside with an axe.

Life at Fort Edmonton

Michel, his wife and children lived in Fort Edmonton during the 1850s. It was built on a relatively high bank, on the north side, overlooking the North Saskatchewan River. The place was like a walled village, as it was surrounded by a palisade. A main gate faced the river and another smaller gate was used to pass things through without having to risk opening it fully. Chief Factor John Rowand had built a baronial mansion called the 'Big House' but most ordinary employees lived in log houses similar to the ones built by the Métis at Lac Ste-Anne. One of the Callihoo boys, Michel, known as "le fou", was certainly born at the Fort on January 25, 1856. Some of the children may have learned to speak English while living here. There was a classroom at Fort Edmonton in 1863, and in 1865, a regular school was opened in the church buildings for twenty pupils with Brother Scollen in charge. It is not known if Michel's child-

Plate 5. Fort Edmonton, 1877 from the south
photo from W.J. Carter Ms, courtesy University of Alberta

ren were there by then nor if they took advantage of the short-lived school at Lac Ste-Anne in the 1870s.

Michel Callihoo achieved the rank of guide for £30 a year in 1859. His brothers, Jean Baptiste, Thomas and Louis worked as middlemen for the Hudson's Bay Company too, but quit after a few years' service. Even Michel didn't sign on at the beginning of 1853, but was hired again in the same year.[38 vi] Perhaps he visited his mother or his father who may have been unwell. They both died in the next year.

A number of Michel's relatives worked for the Company while he was there. Examples are: a son-in-law, Benjamin St. Arneault, brother-in-law, Alexander Savard and a grandnephew, William Rowland. Michel's half-sister, Josephte, and her husband, Charles Beauregard lived at Fort Edmonton for a time. Baptiste L'Hirondelle, a Finlay, a Berland, the Bellerose brothers and Olivier Seguin *dit* Laderoute are other family connections. Michel's married sisters were also in the neighbourhood, at Lac Ste-Anne or St. Albert. In the 1850s, some relatives were known to the Company as freemen, including Pierre Delorme, Michel Patenaude, Louis Loyer and Michel's future father-in-law, Richard Collin.

Clothing

There are no photos of Michel from those days so we know little about how he dressed. However, men of the day wore trousers tied at the knee and ankle, and high or low moccasins. Trousers were often made of wool or other cloth but some people had fine buckskin ones. They might have had outer leggings of blanket cloth attached by buckskin strings to a belt. A man might own a beautiful waistcoat of beaded or embroidered leather, and he wore bright patterned or striped shirts. In addition, a well-dressed man wore a fichu or cravat around his neck and if he had a colourful woven or crocheted sash he didn't need a belt or braces. It was fashionable to wear a decorated hat. A blanket capot (hooded coat) was often worn on top of everything. An alternative was a jacket with brass buttons. Feet were wrapped in cloth, while socks were sometimes worn with manufactured shoes.

Napoleon Callihoo says his Berland grandfather used to keep his tobacco in his sash.

In 1842 Michel obtained a number of red striped shirts and some blue striped shirts as well. He got some corduroy trousers, and a plaid vest. He needed shoes and half hose to wear with them. A silk handkerchief, lace gartering and a red sash finished off the outfit.[38 vi] In 1853, Michel and quite a number of his colleagues treated themselves to new "Canada belts" (probably an Assumption Sash) from the Fort Edmonton stores.[38 i] It must have been a new shipment. You could get buckskin or moleskin trousers from the company store if your wife preferred not to make them. A Métis voyageur might wear a quill-work or beaded leather shot pouch or purse hung over his shoulder by colourful straps as in Paul Kane's painting of François Lucier. He would keep his tobacco and flint in a decorated pouch hanging at his waist. Paul Kane may have been talking about Michel when he described the Métis at a dance at Fort Edmonton in 1855.[40] The men wore beaded leggings, fancy belts and cloth caps with feathers and ribbons. At the turn of the century, Michel was still wearing his hair in a "Dutch" cut, which was a common style many years earlier. Guns and knives were kept in decorated leather cases.

Marie most likely wore dresses trimmed with ribbon on the skirt. Tartan material was very fashionable in those days for dresses and a popular pattern for shawls. Victoria described very elegant girls' leggings of black velvet, beaded on one side.

Sometimes women wore woolen "bloomers" which covered just their thighs. They also wrapped their knees in flannelette against the cold. At the turn of the nineteenth century, some women liked to wear a fine cloak with a red lining and a black fringe.[67 iii] Women and little girls also favoured bead necklaces. Some wore a kerchief or fichu around their necks. A velvet dress was popular for Sundays and weddings. Girls grew their hair long and in braids. The store carried horn combs and ribbons for grown women who wore their long hair pinned up. At boarding school in St. Albert, girls made cotton dresses for every day, but the 'good' dress was dark gingham with a white collar.

Even horses had decorated saddle blankets and harness and sled dogs were fitted out with harness that included embroidery, fringe and bells.

As recently as 1940s, people wore home-made moccasins. They bought rubbers to wear over them. Victoria Callihoo made both one-piece and two-piece moccasins. During hard times, as in the 1890s, women made shirts from flour sacks. In the 1880s, Major Griesbach of Edmonton offered used police uniforms to the Department of Indian Affairs for old people and boys on condition that the jackets be dyed and the buttons removed.

Social Life

Paul Kane was an artist who travelled across the continent in the middle of the nineteenth century. He described some of the activity around Fort Edmonton and told how the Métis families sat around a huge fire of an evening, telling stories, smoking their pipes and enjoying the music played by a fiddler. An inevitable occasion for a ball at the fort was the New Year. When there was a wedding, such as that of John Harriott, a dance and feast were held. Paul Kane tells how everyone from the fort attended, even the local Indians, and everyone danced.[40] Eight- and four-hand reels and jigs were the favoured dances.[54] The Métis men and women sported the most colourful and decorated outfits! It was a very noisy party as there was chatter in many languages all at once and the fiddlers were indefatigable.[40] Michel and all his family likely joined in the dancing there.

Michel and Marie must have led busy social lives. For one thing, people from the fort made frequent visits to family at Lac Ste-Anne. With so many relatives, there were numerous marriages, baptisms and funerals to attend. Some events called for a two-day dance. Two occasions are on record. Michel was an official witness at the marriage of his niece Hélène Beauregard to William Rowland, in 1856, along with John Cunningham, a prominent Hudson's Bay Company employee.[68 xiv] In that same year another well-known Company hunter, Abraham Salois, and Michel formally witnessed the wedding of an old Lesser Slave Lake man, Pierre Laroque.

People loved to dance to the music of the fiddle. To this day, many Métis people enjoy the traditional step dances, jigs and reels of their ancestors. These dances include the famous Red River Jig, the Duck Dance, and Reel of Eight. Somehow everyone managed to squeeze into a house and party all night when there was a wedding or any other excuse to hold a dance, such as a housewarming. If necessary, the dancers moved some of the furniture outside to make room. New Years' celebrations lasted until the sixth of January! Relatives and friends visited back and forth between Lac Ste-Anne, Edmonton and St. Albert. Dances provided a great opportunity for courtship. People very often married relatives, and according to Anne Anderson, older members of the family preferred that young people did so. In some instances there was a dowry which could be sheep, horses or other valuables. Clara Gagnon Dolhagaray said that her mother, Nancy Cunningham, had a dowry.

After a wedding feast and dance, the guests often played pranks on the bride and groom. For instance, guests might hide under a bridge and make weird noises to terrify the horses as the bridal couple drove over. To get the horses to run away was a hilarious joke! Although some people married when they were extremely young, this was not a rule, as one can see from the records. Then, as now, some teenagers had babies before they were married. Relatives usually raised these little ones. Some orphan children were given to the nuns to bring up. For example, when his first wife died in 1887, Jean Felix Callihoo left his two tiny daughters with the Grey Nuns in St. Albert.[2]

When it was time to give birth, a woman skilled in midwifery came in to help. Small babies were bundled with their hands tied down so that they would not scratch their faces. The baby was kept and carried around in a bunting bag lined with moss for insulation. The moss also acted as a disposable diaper. Mothers had to gather a large amount of moss in the fall and store it on the tops of young spruce trees, just tall enough to be above the snow to make it available in the winter. A young baby would get to swing in a sort of blanket hammock strung diagonally across the room. People used to have a remarkable number of children. Although many infants and children died, it was not unusual to have ten live to maturity. Families were commonly augmented by the addition of homeless children. This meant many mouths to feed, but each child had to help with the chores.

Michel and Marie suffered a tragic loss when their little boy, Pierre, died at the age of seven and a daughter, Josephte, when she was only one year old, but had the good fortune to raise their nine other children. At least sixty-seven grandchildren were born.

Working For The Company

The workers at Fort Edmonton were kept busy. In addition to the primary task of dealing with the shipments of goods and furs, they needed to construct or repair buildings and storage facilities and keep the stockade sound. Boats and canoes were built and repaired. Everyone did some carpentry and construction work. Some men, such as Michel, were engaged in travelling and transportation in the summer, while others worked at the fort all year round. Members of the Hodgson family worked as blacksmiths, carpenters and boat builders almost exclusively.

Most Company employees did less skilled work around the place. They sowed, weeded and harvested grain and vegetables. They threshed the grain in order to grind it in a grist mill which operated on wind power. They had to guard the horses, cattle and pigs from theft as well as look after them. The men were very versatile and could fix horse harness, clean barley, pick oakum, make candles and prepare pemmican, to name a few of the skills that were essential to a self-reliant life. Local coal was used at the fort, so they had to mine that, too.

The men were also very competitive. Michel and other packers would compete to see who could carry the heaviest packs. They would first load small ones and then keep adding. Michel was required to help with many tasks and probably learned some new skills over the years. He ran a fishery which brought in extra pay. In addition to their annual wages, most men earned considerable amounts of money by providing the company with hides, dried meat and grease, which their wives probably prepared. Michel also sold the company a work horse for £2 in 1850. Even one of the chief managers, Sir George Simpson, sold moose hides to the Company.

Michel's children with Marie Savard (1828–1869): Hélène (1845–1894) married Benjamin St. Arneault then Francis Colengeard; Pierre (1846–1853); Joseph (1848– ?) married Isabelle Plante; Anne (1850–?) married David Loyer then Pierre Dumont; Olive (1851–?) married Petit Jean Belcourt; Louis (1853–1951) married Rosalie Letendre then Annie Donald; Michel (1856–?) married Mary Jane Donald then Peggy Seguin *dit* Laderoute; Adelaide (1859–?) married Pierre Jean Berland *dit* Valade; Albert (1861–1918) married Marguerite Gladu; Elise (1864–?) married François Boudreau; Josephte (1867–1868).

Each month had its tasks: maintaining the post and preparing for the summer work ahead. In January, Michel built and repaired horse sleds. He also ground some barley with a steel mill. This was the season to cut more firewood for his own house. There were so many people at Fort Edmonton that providing food for them all was a constant preoccupation of the post managers. In 1852, there were forty men, thirty women and eighty children living at the fort. In the 1850s the daily ration for a man was eight pounds of fresh meat, and two to three pounds of pemmican or dried meat. The women and children also received rations.

Michel took some men with him to Lac Ste-Anne to fish one January. They returned in a few days with 1017 whitefish on eight sledges. The total annual fishery was 10,000—much of it to feed the dogs. This was described as a shortfall of about 20,000 fish! In 1861, he was sent with thirty horses toward the plains to look for bison. He returned with a disappointing 9800 pounds of meat, thirty tongues and twenty robes, saying that the horses were 'too poor'. His boss remarked that the employees were at fault for not hunting hard enough as they were ordered to do. He claimed that they wasted their time visiting the freemen's camp, instead.[38i]

In February, Michel was back to repairing both dog and horse sleds. It was also the time to chop wood for oars. They then had to be shaped and planed. It might have taken over a month of work to get them right. In 1859, he took the oxen out to get ice that was then cut up in the ice house and stored in an ice cellar. One year, Michel collected bark for labels, which were called "tickets", for the packs of fur. These were stamped with "brands" made by the blacksmith.[38i]

In March he finished up the oars and did various kinds of construction work. In 1854, he pulled down a store, sawed couplers (roof rafters) for the new Indian House and laid flooring in it. By 1861, the house needed new floor boards in the garret, which Michel hauled with horses from the sawing tent and then installed. He was in charge of carrying enough wood for the new "French" church with ten horses. In 1856, it fell to him to pull down an old storage building. He helped pack furs and moved furs and meat from the trading shop to the fur store. One year, Michel had to meet the stage (we don't know where it came from) and bring home some eight cows and ten horses. Another year he took bison tongues out of 'pickle',

Plate 6. Hauling boat (tracking) up Athabasca River, n.d.
photo from W.J. Carter Ms, courtesy University of Alberta

that is, out of the salt brine in which they had soaked for some twenty days and hung them up in the mess hall. They preserved 360 tongues in this way at one time. On March 17, 1859, Michel dug a trench so that ground temperature could be measured in order to plan for the vegetable garden. At times, he also had to make pemmican and cut cordwood.[38i]

Early in April one year, Michel rode with a party of five men and ten horses to the Plains for meat. They returned empty-handed within a week because the horses gave out half way. In other years, in the month of April, he made fences for the fields, and enclosed a little store with pickets as well. In this month, he found birch for canoes, squared some logs and worked on the old men's house. He also finished his oars and made sweeps for the boats. After the season's furs were in from the outlying posts to this central location, many people were engaged in compacting and packing them. There were also buffalo robes to be packed. In April 1860, Michel was sent to look for a boat that had somehow been lost.[38i]

During the spring, men prepared the boats for the heavy service they would have to provide all summer long. By May, it was getting close to the time to ship out. Michel regularly voyaged as far as Winnipeg and back. In addition to bark canoes, York boats were used.

Around the 1820s, 'York' boats were being built and used to a greater degree and were preferred by the Hudson's Bay Company because they were sturdier, safer, and could carry more cargo. These were modified Orkney Islands whaleboats, 28 feet long by six feet wide. They could be propelled with oars, a tracking line, or large square sails. They were sailed with rudders or a long sweep. By the 1850s, York boats were used almost exclusively. These were built right at Fort Edmonton and required skilled craftsmen. In a typical spring, along with other steersmen, such as his brother-in-law Antoine Savard, Michel prepared oars and made masts. They caulked and pitched the boats for days to make them waterproof. They cleaned the canvas and the leather sails. The packs of fur had to be carried down to the river. In 1859, Michel was in the first brigade of four boats which left on the twelfth of May. In another year, they might still have been making packs at that time.[38i]

Michel shipped out later in some years. In June, he could have been hauling logs up the hill from the river, sawing stockades, taking them to the fort with his brother Thomas, or constructing buildings. He was still doing this sort of thing in mid-July, 1865. On July 9, 1862, while Michel was at Fort Pitt, he was asked to guide a party of Overlanders (a group of British Gold seekers, heading for the Cariboo) to Fort Edmonton. He took them across the Saskatchewan River and by the southerly trail to the Fort.[91]

In August, Michel was usually away from Fort Edmonton. On 18 August, 1863, he made it back from Red River. The return trip took 55 days and the party had nearly been robbed by some Cree on the way home. In 1869 and 1870, he was in charge of a brigade which was to take furs down to Fort Carlton by boat and return in August with goods and supplies loaded on ox carts. His boss remarked in his journal that he was very satisfied to find the goods all in fine condition and that they matched the lists exactly.[38i]

The last boats returned in September one year Michel reached the fort on the twentieth. He also delivered the outfit for the outlying Company posts. He went to Rocky Mountain House, on one occasion and to Lac Ste-Anne, another. In the fall, people started to prepare for the winter by 'mudding' their houses, that is, filling the chinks between the logs.[38i]

Michel and his brothers also plastered the church and priest's house, inside and out, in October 1859. October was a busy month for Michel because he was in charge of the fishery established at Lac Ste-Anne in 1856. Henry J. Moberley said that Michel, the Head Fisherman, was sent to Lac Ste-Anne to "hang up" thirty thousand whitefish.[53] The fish were netted, cleaned, split and suspended in the air from poles to dry and thus would have kept all winter. Michel went regularly to the plains to hunt at this time of year, as well as attending to the fishery, even in December.[38i]

In between all their activities, employees had to find time to look after their own families. There wasn't enough food at the Fort in 1861, so the men were allowed to go fishing to supply food for their families. Some freemen, probably from the west, arrived in Edmonton bringing furs but they too were short of food. Hard times had already begun. People were said to be starving at Lac La Biche. At Fort Edmonton they were disappointed again, this time with the amount of bison obtained from a hunt near Rocky Mountain House—so much so that they were obliged to kill some of their draft animals (oxen) for food. Even Michel's brother-in-law, the interpreter Olivier Bellerose, along with his family of about ten children, nearly starved in the summer of 1860. He hired on to winter again in 1861, on the condition that he be provided with provisions. Olivier used dogs for winter freighting and needed fish to feed them, too.[38i]

Sometime in the 1860s, Michel, his wife and their nine children moved back to Lac Ste-Anne where he and his brother Jean Baptiste continued to manage the fishery for the Hudson's Bay Company. After 1863, Michel Callihoo was described as "guide and fish" in the account book. He now had more responsibility. He was put in charge of the Fort Pitt brigade in 1870.[37i] Michel retired for good in 1873.

Disease and Danger

Those who described the simple conditions of life in the nineteenth century spoke of happy, busy times. They did not mention the very crowded little houses, the numbers of babies who died or how hungry you could get. When fish and game were scarce, people actually starved. You might have lost half your children from measles or diphtheria and two-thirds of the family could have died of the dreaded smallpox, which visited the area with a vengeance in 1870.

The pursuit of bison was a dangerous activity, though your neighbours might have given you even more trouble. For instance, Father Lacombe was wounded in the chest during the fight which ensued when some Blackfoot surprised his Cree travelling companions at midnight on December 3, 1865.[30] John Cunningham's trip to the Plains, in 1866, was a failure because some Blackfoot plundered the carts and would have killed the whole party had they not been deterred by the presence of some Blood and Peigan Indians.[37i]

The wooden houses people lived in were extremely susceptible to fire, especially as they used grease candles or kerosene for light. Drowning was also not uncommon. Michel Callihoo's youngest brother, Louis, met his death this way near Fort Assiniboine.[34] Some people were accidentally shot by mishandling guns. That was how Edward Berland *dit* Valade's two sons died while duck hunting in 1863.

Medicines made from wild herbs were the only ones available, apart from a few potions sold by the Hudson's Bay Company. Knowledgeable women had learned when and where to look for plants. In addition, they knew what they could do for a sick person and how best to prepare and administer the drugs. Examples include ginger root (rat root) which is good for sore throats when chewed but as an infusion works to soothe an earache. High bush cranberry bark is a pain reliever, mint tea helps to bring down a fever, wintergreen is good against kidney stones, strawberry leaves and stems help relieve dysentery, boiled green spruce cones are good for scabies and Lady Slippers can be taken for female disorders. Bulrush roots served as a poultice on open sores. On occasion, people also tried 'magic' cures with some success.

Religion

Christian clergy played an important role in the communities of Métis people. Methodist ministers, James Evans and Robert Rundle, began to convert people at settlements on the North Saskatchewan River and at Lesser Slave Lake before a Roman Catholic Mission was even established at Lac Ste-Anne in 1843. Father Lacombe, a member of the Oblate order later remarked that 're-conversion' was necessary. One example was Hélène Beauregard, Michel Callihoo's neice. She was baptized by Robert Rundle, in 1841,[76] and again by an Oblate priest in 1842.[68 xiv] While there were some early Protestant communities in central Alberta, such as the Victoria Settlement, Lac Ste-Anne and St. Albert remained essentially Roman Catholic in the nineteenth century.

Father Lacombe said that the people lived in the manner of the Indians and described his efforts to change the behaviour of these gambling, drinking, and merry-making people by discouraging hand-game gambling and by forming a Temperance Society in 1853.[43]

Albert Lacombe was the priest and mentor at Lac Ste-Anne from 1853 until he established a mission at St. Albert in 1861. Three Sisters of Charity called Grey Nuns, Sisters Zoë Leblanc-Emery, Marie Jacques-Alphonse and Adèle Lamy followed the Oblates to Lac Ste-Anne in 1859. There the Sisters started a school but also left for St. Albert soon after. Christine Lacombe, who was Father Lacombe's sister, came to Lac Ste-Anne as

Plate 7. Michel Callihoo's sister, Angelique, and her husband, Louis Loyer ca.1905 *courtesy Lorraine McDonald*

Plate 8. *from left:* Jeanne Callioux, Alexander Savard, Norbert Callioux, Louis (Michel Callihoo's son), Mrs. Savard, ca. 1925
courtesy Musée Héritage Museum

the school teacher from 1871–1873. After this, however, opportunities for an education were poor as the next teacher did not arrive until 1879.[26] Thus, a whole generation at Lac Ste-Anne lacked a chance to learn to read and write.

New Family

Michel's wife, Marie Savard, died in 1869, and in 1870, Michel married Philomène Collin who was about half his age. She had been baptized at Lesser Slave Lake, a daughter of Richard Collin who was a previous fur trade employee, born in Moose Factory. Collin worked out of Jasper House, but after he got married lived as a freeman in the region of the Smoky River. Philomène's mother was Geneviève, a daughter of a Jean Baptiste Bruyères and Françoise Serpent. By 1874, Philomène's dad was a widower living at Lac Ste-Anne where some of his ten children lived, too. A few of them became Michel's relatives by marriage. For example, Philomène's nephew Jean Felix Gladu married Michel's niece, Cécile Belcourt.

With all these relatives, Michel and Philomène must have had many social obligations. Michel was godfather to his grandson, Norbert Callihoo, born and baptized in 1875. In the 1880s alone, Michel and Philomène could have attended the baptisms of more than twenty grandchildren, and the marriages or baptisms of another twenty nieces and nephews.

There were funerals as well. For example, Michel lost two sisters and two brothers between 1865 and 1874, while Philomène's father passed away in 1877. Michel and Philomène's first child died in 1870 at only ten months, possibly of smallpox, and another four-year-old son died in 1891, during another epidemic of the disease. However, they successfully raised ten more children and at least one grandson to maturity.

Richard Collin (1793–1877) and Geneviève Bruyères (1815–1865) had the following children: Catherine (1825–?) married Joseph Paquette; Sophie (1827–?) married Jean Baptiste Gladu; James (1834–?) married Judith Godin; Richard (1839–?) married Nancy Berland; Jeanne (1840–1912) married Jean Dorian Gladu then a St. Arneault; Henry (1842–?) married Elise Cameron; Isabelle (1845–?) married William Berland; Philomène (1848–1932) married Michel Callihoo; Mathias "Muchas" (1853–1939).

By 1874, the census at Lac Ste-Anne gives us some idea of the composition of the community. There were 41 families counted, nearly half of whom were First Nations people (mostly Assiniboine). Michel Callihoo and two of his brothers lived here at this time with their wives and children. In the other houses were their adult children who had started families of their own. Most of the rest were very closely related to each other. For instance, Baptiste L'Hirondelle and his wife, Catherine Loyer, lived in a house with five of their younger children, an adult son and his teenaged wife, Euphrasine. This girl was a Beauregard and was a niece of Michel Callihoo. Catherine's brother, Louis Loyer, lived nearby with his wife, Angélique, who was Michel's sister. Another sister's son, Philip Gray, lived with them. One household was composed of Michel Callihoo's sister, Cécile, her second husband, Edward Berland, three of their small children and Edward's grown son, Pierre Jean. Her Belcourt children lived with their eldest brother, his young wife and their baby. Their uncle Alexis Belcourt and his family including young Victoria were members of this same community. Michel's widowed daughter, Hélène, lived at Lac Ste-Anne as did numerous in-laws of the Richard Collin family.

Although Michel was retired and no doubt had a pension, he took employment where he could find it. He and his grown sons were paid by the Mission at Lac Ste-Anne for occasional work.[68x] In 1876, Michel received $9.50; his sons Louis $10.70, Michel $4.50, and young Albert $5.00. Various people made money providing such commodities as cordwood, pemmican or fish, and services such as labouring and freighting. The account book doesn't say exactly what the Callihoos, in particular, were doing for the money. The family also bought things from the Mission. In 1877, Michel paid them $2.50 and Louis was paid $12.50 in goods. His wife earned $1.50 this year. Had she made some moccasins?

Michel's children with Philomène Collin (1848–1932): Elzéar (1870–1870); Marie (1871–1956) spouses unknown; Josephine (1872–?) married Joseph Laderoute *dit* Seguin; Solomon Emile (1874–1967) married Elizabeth Plante; James (1877–1935) married Marie Louise L'Hirondelle; Isabelle (1879–?) married Joseph Perrault then Charles Guppie; Christina (1881–?) married Archie Fife; Johnny (1884–1957) married Sophie Cunningham; Felix (1885–?); François (1887–1891); Corinne (1889–?) married Albert, Conte de Pierpont; Emmaline (1894–1978) married Willie Dubis.

St. Albert and Lac Ste-Anne Afterwards

When the new Mission at St. Albert was founded in 1861, a number of families, such as the Beaudrys, moved from Lac Ste-Anne to take advantage of the better farm land there. The St. Albert census of 1872 describes a population of 285 men, 312 women and 805 children, mostly "half-breeds" and some Cree. No 'whites' are mentioned. Among those who moved to St. Albert in 1875 are the L'Hirondelles, the father and some of his sons, the Chastellaines, the Belcourts and the Cunninghams. Some of these men were still in the employ of the Hudson's Bay Company while others were freemen. Some Métis people from Red River also came west to the St. Albert area. The population of Lac Ste-Anne was down to 156 people in 1879, while St. Albert eventually grew into a city.

Lac Ste-Anne became famous again as an important site for pilgrimage and healing. For over a century Native people have made an annual visit to the old mission and lake. They travelled in horse-drawn vehicles and camped in tents for a week. Later, there was an excursion train to take people from St. Albert to the pilgrimage. One year the train derailed, killing some people. Nowadays pilgrims drawn from as far as the Northwest Territories and the United States bring their motorhomes and campers.

When Michel settled at Lac Ste-Anne he built a fine house that was later described by the Surveyor, G.A. Simpson, who was visiting the West to survey Reserve lands. He wrote, "At the head of the Lake is the present home of the Chief. He has a comfortable house, size 20′ × 26′, hall running through the center and rooms on each side. His outbuildings which consist of Storehouse, 12′ × 16′ stable with stalls for cattle and horses, calf pens and hay loft, are all in good repair. He has about twelve acres fenced and under cultivation, and seems to be doing his best to make a comfortable living."[23 iii]

Michel's granddaughter says that when he lived at Lac Ste-Anne, her grandfather walked around the lake shore to get to Mass on Sunday, in order to avoid going out in a boat. His wife would leave later and row the children over. Had Michel developed an aversion to water? Was it a penance?

Michel Becomes a Chief

Michel decided to move his family from Lac Ste-Anne to live on an Indian Reserve. As Father Albert Lacombe O.M.I., wrote in 1878:[68 ii]

> Sept 23 Lundi—neige fondante—ce matin arrivé du courrier. ... Le traité de nos sauvages est complétement temoiné; toute une bande de métis du Lac Ste-Anne sont entrés dans le traité, et ont pour chef, Michel Calliot." [September 23 Monday—snow melting—this morning mail came. ... The Treaty of our Indians is completely witnessed a whole band of Métis from Lac Ste-Anne have entered in the Treaty and have as Chief, Michel Callihoo.] (See chapter III.)

This decision, which very much affected the future of Michel's and his brother's families, may have been taken from a strong sense of responsibility in the face of economic uncertainty in rapidly changing times. This plan for the future demonstrates Michel's impressive leadership qualities and forethought.

Michel took a financial loss when he abandoned his house for the Reserve. As Simpson said in his letter describing the Alexis Reserve on Lac Ste-Anne: "As the Eastern Boundary of this Reserve, according to the Chief's location, was only about two miles west of Michel's buildings and clearing, and as they will be abandoned next year, I thought it better to go still further east and include them in Alexis' Reserve. I would respectfully suggest, in consideration of Michel leaving his buildings as they are at present, that some remuneration in the way of nails, glass, hinges, and a few days work, be given him to assist in putting up his new premises."[23 iii] Michel was quite willing to allow Chief Alexis to take possession. In fact, he seemed better pleased with the idea than Alexis himself, who said he was afraid he would be called upon to pay for the house and is quoted as saying "he had nothing to pay with." Although Michel claimed $1000, Simpson thought the improvements were worth about $200 and told Michel that the government would make good the loss.[22 iii] A letter from E.J. Galt, a federal employee, on Oct. 26, 1881, recommended a cheque be sent to Chief Michel. A reply to Galt on November 22 said that it would be better for the Department if they were to "merely assist Chief Calihoo" in his building operations in his new Reserve by supplying him with such articles as window sashes, doors, nails and boards. The letter went on to say, "You will therefore instruct the Indian Agent to render such assistance to Chief 'Calihoo' when he has his buildings in such a state of progress as will warrant the same being done." Michel ended up with material worth only $44.49.[23 ii]

Simpson said that Callihoo intended abandoning the improvements made by him at Lac Ste-Anne as he did not like the soil, "it being light, and he was eager to get near white settlement in order that he might acquaint himself with the white man's mode of living".[23 iii] If Michel really said this, he was surely being disingenuous because he must have been very well acquainted with this mode of living, after all those years employed with the Hudson's Bay Company in Edmonton. According to the Indian Act, a band could pretty well choose the reserve property from available Crown land. Nearly a hundred years later, Joseph Dion wrote that Michel chose to sign Treaty because of the good hunting on the reserve lands.[25]

Michel was now entitled to special clothing. In 1882, in the Edmonton region, a chief got a blue coat with gold on the collar, matching trousers, blue flannel shirts, and also silk handkerchiefs, leather belts, woolen socks and high laced Blucher boots. He could also have a felt hat with a gold band. The Headman, Joseph Gladu, was given a blue cloth jacket faced with red and other clothes. Michel, as chief, was also supposed to get a medal, a flag, in addition to a horse, harness and wagon.

Michel and Philomène eventually settled at the Reserve with six young children, in 1883. They built a two-storey house right on the Lac Ste-Anne Trail in a natural hay meadow. They also built barns and out-buildings. Two of Michel's sons with his first wife, Joseph and Michel, did not live on the Reserve, but young Louis said he farmed there for a while, before moving north. Joseph was paying for a place in the cemetery in 1891–1892 and shopped at the Mission, so he must have lived near St. Albert.[68 xii] He later moved to St. Paul des Métis. Young Michel moved to near Rivière-Qui-Barre, where he owned a quarter section in the 1880s and he too was paying for a place in the St. Albert cemetery. Michel's daughter, Hélène Colengeard, was living in St. Albert when she died in

---

An impression gained from talking to his descendants is that Chief Michel is a hero to the family because he asserted and maintained their Aboriginal heritage and rights by signing Treaty.

1894. There was a splendid "grand service", which cost $15.00 for her funeral, in September and two grand masses, at only $2.50, later in the year.[68 xii] The youngest brother of the first family, Albert, married the Headman's daughter, Marguerite Gladu, and made his home on the Reserve with a family of about ten children until his untimely death in 1918, of Spanish Influenza. Of Michel's daughters with Marie, Adelaide and her husband, Pierre Jean Berland, did move to the Reserve and stayed there. By 1903, Michel's adult sons of his second family still lived on the Reserve while most of the adult sons of his brother Jean Baptiste and some grandsons were active in Band affairs. The Indian agent reported that the chief and his brother had as fine places as any white settler.

Michel, the Man

What do we know of Michel Callihoo, the man? He was a reliable worker and worthy of respect, judging from the Hudson's Bay Company journals. He had risen to positions of authority in the ranks of that Company. The government Surveyor George Simpson said he was intelligent and although Michel could neither read nor write, he was able to speak Cree, French and English. He was a great believer in education for his children for he sent them to the best school he could, even though, as his family remembers, it was far away and he missed them badly. Michel was also somewhat of an opportunist. Proof of this came in 1885, when he presented himself before the Half-Breed Claims Commission, with the documentation required to obtain half-breed money scrip ($240 worth) as the legitimate heir of his baby son, Elzéar, who had died fifteen years earlier.[23 xxi]

He was a pious man and was baptized a Roman Catholic as soon as there was an opportunity. He and his family could regularly attend the church he had helped build in Fort Edmonton in 1857. He paid for two expensive grand masses to be sung at Lac Ste-Anne in November 1870.[68 viii] Religious observances were often combined with fun. The family may have attended the St. Jean Baptiste celebration in St. Albert in June 1889. On this Holy Day after Mass they held a dinner, then a picnic with running races and horse races, ending up with a dance. Michel generously provided lumber for the church of St. Peter at Villeneuve and

Plate 9. Jean Baptiste Callihoo's sons, unidentified, with wives ca. 1900
photo Ernest Brown, Provincial Archives of Alberta

Plate 10. *from left:* Philomène Callihoo, Sévère Callihoo, Michel Callihoo, unknown priest, Jean Baptiste Callihoo, 3 unidentified ladies
courtesy Musée Héritage Museum

Plate 11. St. Joseph's Industrial School, High River, 1888. At least eight of these children are Callihoos. Second from the left, seated, may be Solomon. *Provincial Archives of Alberta*

brought his family regularly when it was built. His daughter, Christina, was married here in 1899.

As an important man, Michel participated in special religious events. When Archbishop Taché came from Winnipeg to Alberta in August of 1888, a great celebration took place at the Alexander Reserve. Men on horseback fired off a salute with their guns. Chiefs Michel and Alexander sat with the dignitaries and talked to the eminent visitor. When a set of bells were dedicated and blessed on this occasion, Michel's wife, Philomène was named one of the "godparents" of the bells.[68 i]

Near the End of the Century

Even on the Reserve, people were having to make plans for a different economic future. One way was to learn to read and write and acquire new skills. A number of Michel's young children and his grandson, William, were educated at St. Joseph's Industrial School, also called Dunbow, at High River. Josephine left home to board there when she was twelve, in November 1885, accompanied by her brothers, eleven-year-old Solomon and little James, who was barely eight. She was a most responsible girl and by 1888 was given the task of teaching the other girls to bake. She stayed at the school for a little over five years achieving a level five (the highest level) and was labelled "proficient". They also said, "We expect that she will easily find a position as a servant girl." She ended up teaching school! Solomon was an outstanding student and was therefore chosen to deliver a special welcome to the Lieutenant Governor, Mr. Dewdney, during his visit to the school on March 15, 1886. Young Solomon must have been quite a hit reading from an illuminated scroll on this occasion. The child was rewarded in August with a trip to Calgary accompanying the carpenter, Picard. James got to go the following year with Father Claude. Each year their dad came down to visit them in May bringing another child to enroll. Next to start school was Isabelle who was discharged at the top level when she was only fourteen. One May, Michel was back again with the whole family to see his children. He had to wait around until early June because the Commissioner of Indian Affairs couldn't decide whether or not to accept one of them.[68 vi]

On January 1 of 1890, it was nine-year-old Christina's turn to get up and contribute to the ceremonies by reciting a short piece after which they all sang *Auld Lang Syne*. Four years later she was removed from the school in order to go to the convent in St. Albert. Johnny, too, left Dunbow at eleven to finish his schooling closer to home.[68 vi] In 1891, the Inspector of Agencies for Indian Affairs reported, among other things, that those who had been to High River School spoke good English. What he didn't know was that some of Michel's children already spoke English by the time they went to school as they had already achieved Level One at the time of enrolment. This is difficult to account for unless perhaps their parents used English at home when they didn't want the children to understand what they were saying. Maybe it didn't work and the children picked up the language. The three youngest children went to the industrial school in St. Albert.

Chief Michel had a farm and owned his own mower, horse, rake and reaper. He is described in the Edmonton Bulletin of November 14, 1885 as the largest grain farmer on the Reserve. It should be understood that people who had the means had commercial dealings, separate from those of the collectivity. Michel also dealt in horses and other livestock, but this could be hazardous. When Michel was thrown from a horse in November 1890, he broke his collarbone. The Indian Agent got him a doctor and remarked that the sixty-five-year-old man was already visiting him in Edmonton at Christmas—which seems a remarkable recovery.[23 xiii] Like other businessmen, Michel had tardy creditors. He had to engage a lawyer to bring Ludger Bellerive of St. Albert to court in August 1895, for a payment of $15.00 plus interest still outstanding on a mare and colt sold for $35.00.[83]

Michel was an entrepreneur as well as successful farmer. He remained in the freighting business after leaving the Company. One of his deals was reported in the newspaper on June 2, 1883: "Michel Callihou started down the river to Prince Albert on Friday with a raft of 34 M [thousand] feet of rough lumber from the Hudson's Bay Company mills and 4000 feet of dressed lumber from the Edmonton mills."

Michel kept some of his old shopping habits for years. He and his sons continued to trade at the Hudson's Bay Company store in Edmonton. In

1887, he paid a debt of $15.00, and still had an account with them in 1903, when his son Felix went in for tea, gunpowder, shot and caps. On the other hand, Michel's sons, Joseph and Michel, and a few other relatives who lived in St. Albert got some of their things from the Mission. They often paid in grain. Michel also patronized Hebert and Perron General Store in St. Albert after the turn of the century. He not only obtained goods, but was trusted enough to be advanced cash. His sons and his brother, Jean Baptiste, shopped here, too.

When the Duke of Cornwall and York (later King George V) made a ceremonial visit to Calgary on September 28, 1901, Michel probably went to Calgary to attend, because the Treaty medals were handed out on this occasion. Another medal was received for attendance at the ceremony. The affair was thronged by a thousand Indians decorated with paint and feathered headdresses. In addition to receiving medals, each chief had a chance to make a speech and to meet the Duke and Duchess.

After the turn of the century the business of the Reserve was very trying. There were ongoing negotiations to obtain funds to update machinery and equipment, resulting in surrenders of land. It became so difficult to deal with the government officials that the Band wanted to quit Treaty for a deal of land and cash.

At the End

Michel became ill in 1910 and for a while Reserve affairs were confused. It didn't help to have his brother, and lifetime companion, Jean Baptiste, die in that year. Michel himself died on April 8, 1911. His son, Solomon, made his coffin, and arranged for his parents to rest in the churchyard cemetery in St. Albert. The original wooden crosses have since been replaced with newer gravestones.

Michel would certainly have been gratified, had he lived, to know that the school south of the Michel Reserve was named the Michael School in his memory. His son James, grandson Daniel and three nephews were

---

It is said that Michel's son Albert was so shy that when he went shopping in St. Albert with his wife, he would stay in the wagon while she made the purchases—even for his clothes. It was also said of him, "If he had no shoes, he would walk to church barefoot."

involved in the rate-payers' association and Vital Victor, a grand-nephew, was elected as a trustee to the first board of the new Michael School District in 1928.

About ten years after her husband's death, Philomène moved to St. Albert where she lived with her daughter, Marie. She received a pension, probably from the Hudson's Bay Company. They were joined by Philomène's brother, 'Muchas', in his retirement. Philomène died on February 21, 1932, and is buried next to Michel.

IN
LOVING MEMORY
OF
OUR BELOVED FATHER
MICHAEL CALLIOU.
BORN OCT. 1. 1823.
DIED APRIL 6. 1911.
AGED 88 YEARS.
BELOVED HUSBAND OF
PHILOMENE COLLINS
R. I. P.

Plate 12. Michel Callihoo's grave in St. Albert Cemetery
photo Elizabeth Macpherson

MICHEL RESERVE #132

In 1876, numerous Indian bands living in what are now known as Alberta and Saskatchewan signed Treaty #6, mainly at Fort Carlton and Fort Pitt. Michel Callihoo signed this document on behalf of his "Cree band" of Métis relatives and connections on September 23 of 1878.

The British Government had made treaties with various First Nations for about a hundred years prior to this. These were essentially peace treaties. The Treaties were deemed to extinguish further land claims by the Aboriginal tribal groups who signed them. Treaty #6 was one of these agreements between Indian Nations and the Crown and states that the Indians "will maintain peace and good order between each other, and between themselves and other tribes of Indians and between themselves and others of Her Majesty's subjects." However, it is more than just a peace treaty. Those who signed Treaty became Status Indians under the Indian Act which was then and is still administered by a Canadian Government department. As such, the people of a so-called band of Indians were to make their homes on designated lands called 'reserves', which the members of the Band held in common. The band's finances were controlled by the Department of Indian Affairs whose hierarchy consisted of a local Indian Agent and various ranks of civil servants answerable ultimately to a Cabinet Minister in Ottawa. By signing Treaty #6, Indians were deprived of the franchise which in the 1870s was available to any other adult who owned the requisite amount of property. Each Status Indian received a small annuity for life, paid no taxes, and liquor was not allowed on the reserves nor was it permitted to sell it to Indians. Since

There were subsequent signings known as "adhesions" by various other bands in subsequent years. For instance, a band of Stony Indians also living at Lac Ste-Anne had already signed an adhesion to Treaty #6 in 1877 under Chief Alexis.

then, the Indian Act has been changed. Status Indians have had the right to vote in federal elections since 1960.

Why did the Métis freeman, Michel Callihoo, sign Treaty? One important reason may have been that this was an opportunity to obtain a large tract of excellent land, free of charge. The soil was especially fertile. It was a good place to hunt, fish and trap as well. There was also a good deal of timber. Although some people were still able to live by hunting and trapping, there really was little option in this period of declining game but to attempt agriculture. Accordingly, the Treaty promised that farm equipment and livestock would be provided by the government. There were other incentives and benefits. In addition to a cash payment in perpetuity of five dollars annually for each person there was an initial gift of \$12.00. Chiefs and headmen were to get \$25 and \$15 respectively per year. Treaty #6 also promised medical care, free education and relief in hard times. Nearly unlimited hunting and fishing were to be permitted on reserves and unoccupied Crown Land, with \$1500 to be provided each year for ammunition for hunting and for twine to make fish nets.[14] Michel and his clan could not have expected that the terms of the Treaty would not all be honoured, nor could they have predicted the excessive paternalism practised by the Canadian Government.

Band Members

At the time he took Treaty Michel made his home at Lac Ste-Anne with his second wife and four small children. A few of his adult children and grandchildren lived there as well. His brothers, Thomas and Jean Baptiste, and his sisters, Cécile Berland and Angélique Loyer, and their families were at Lac Ste-Anne, too. Some of these relatives and a few other families from this small community chose to join Michel in the Treaty. Michel's younger brother, Jean Baptiste, with whom he was very close, signed on. His half-brothers and sisters may have been included but did not move to the Reserve. Michel's grown sons, Joseph, Louis and Michel, and daughters, Hélène St. Arneault, Adelaide Berland Valade, and Anne Dumont, counted themselves in. Some Collin in-laws signed Treaty, too. Only a few relatives and connections of the Callihoos who lived at Lac Ste-Anne, such as the L'Hirondelles and the Belcourts, signed Treaty.

Father Lacombe spoke of some orphans whom the Sisters at Ile à la Crosse wanted included in the Treaty. It isn't known what happened to them in the end, but this illustrates the casualness concerning what constituted an Indian band in those days. In any event, there were numerous families called "stragglers" by the government who signed Treaty and were added to various bands, including Michel's. Members of the Campion and Chalifoux families were in this category and were paid as Band members by the Department of Indian Affairs. They later disappeared from the list. The family of a Michel Cardinal and some Hamelins were paid their Treaty annuity for a time.[23 xx] Most stragglers never lived on the Reserve.

Michel Callihoo's so-called Cree Band originally consisted of 48 families. According to the Indian agent's report on elections for Michel's band, the chief and Joseph Gladu, Headman, were elected in 1880 and they were there for life. Treaty #6 provided for one square mile for each family of five or 128 acres per person. Transcripts from the Department of Indian Affairs show that 178 people were on the pay list in 1878, the first year; as many as 231 were on it the following year and in 1880 there were only 155. Half of these people left Treaty over the next ten years. Amongst those who quit were Michel's sister, Cécile, as well as his sons and a daughter from his first family. A couple of Jean Baptiste's sons, Jean Felix and John, also obtained their discharges and took scrip. Louis Courtereille, a signatory of the actual Treaty document, quit in 1885 and most of his daughters married and moved away.[23 xxi]

In 1885 alone fifty members withdrew from Michel's Band and applied to take up the Halfbreed Commission's offer of scrip. By 1890, the population of the Reserve was officially down to 76 people. This made the acreage they were entitled to upon signing only 9,728 acres from the original 22,784. There was an attempt to repossess some of the land when the population went down, but according to the Indian Act, the Department did not have the power to reduce reserves.[86]

The forty-square-mile Michel Reserve was originally surveyed in September 1880 by G.A. Simpson, the government surveyor. It is a lovely

---

Some say the term "stragglers" refers to people who missed the Treaty signing occasion and finally did sign, late.

place. Along the eastern and southern boundaries it was then partially wooded with poplar and fir, while along the western boundary and the Sturgeon River it was more heavily timbered. Nearly half of the Reserve is high rolling prairie and the soil is clay loam, described as "of the choicest quality". There is plenty of water with some small lakes and the Sturgeon River and Atim Creek. You could catch such fish as pike and 'Marias' (ling) and there were moose, deer and much small game such as grouse and hare. Muskrat, beaver, mink, marten and lynx could be trapped for the fur market.

One by one, families packed their belongings into wagons and left their old homes to take over the new property in the early 1880s. A few lived in bark teepees while they cut trees and cleared land. They went on to construct log cabins, barns and fences. The houses built of large hewn logs had dovetailed corners and dormer windows in a high pitched roof. Some of the houses, barns, corrals and seeded fields were located right on the old Lac Ste-Anne Trail from Edmonton. The Band had not built a bridge over the seasonal creek in front of their buildings. This was in order to prevent a regular right-of-way through the Reserve for users of the Lac Ste-Anne Trail west, according to Mr. J. Priestly, who is also quoted as saying that "Chief Calahoo and his wife were very sociable to passers-by, whom they treated to good meals and comfortable lodging."[1]

The Department of Indian Affairs distributed some bulls, cows, oxen and horses amongst the then five reserves of the Edmonton region. It was

---

The report of the surveyor of the reserve Simpson, reads, "It is bounded by a line beginning at a post on the right bank of the Sturgeon River, twenty-six chains and forty links, more or less, north, and forty-six chains and eighty-seven links, more or less, west of the south-east corner of section thirty-one, township fifty-four, range twenty-six, west of the fourth initial meridian, and running south six hundred chains and thirty-seven links, more or less, to a post thence west four hundred chains, more or less, to a post thence north six hundred and eighty-seven chains and seven links, more or less, to a post on the right bank of the Sturgeon River and thence easterly along the said bank of the said river to the point of beginning, containing an area of forty square miles more or less."

There is no evidence that the Reserve lands once extended as far as the Rocky Mountains nor that this was in some way ancestral land of the Callihoos, as asserted by Robert Callihoo.[10]

EDMONTON SHEET

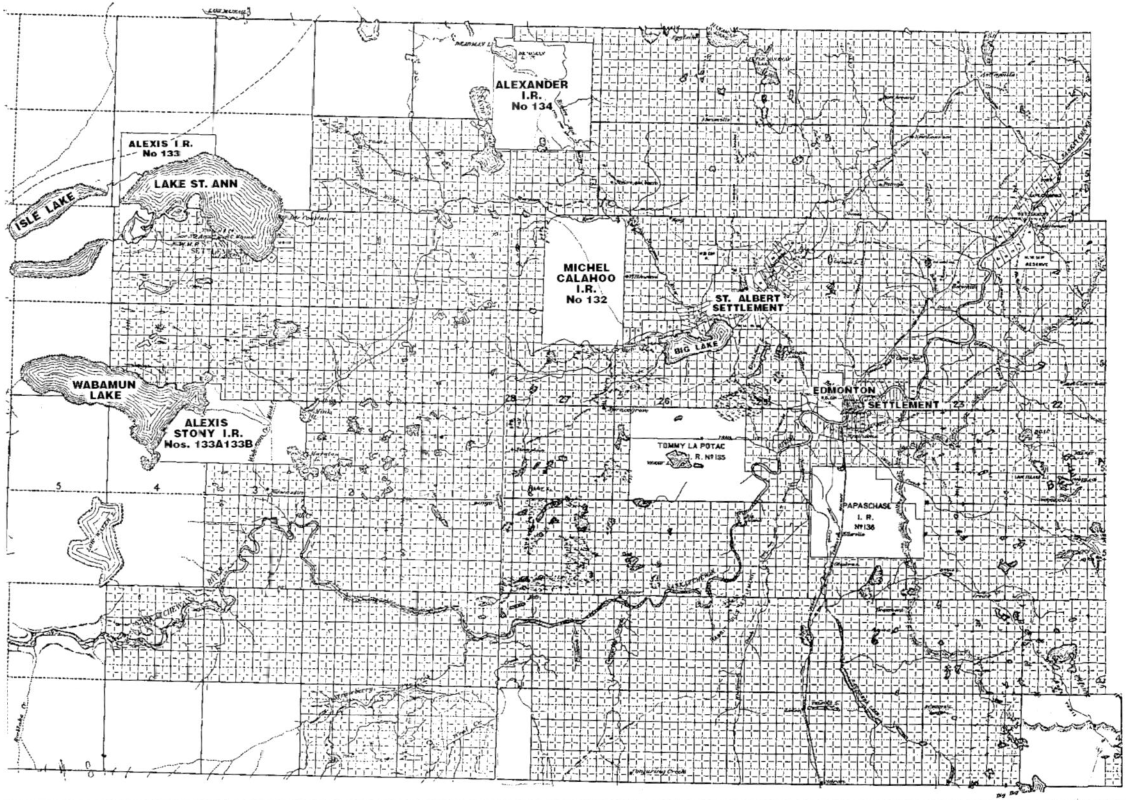

Plate 13. Copy of Surveyor General sheets, #s 79 and 314, 1903, 1904, scale: 1:800 000 approx.

TREATY
1876

Plate 14. Beatrice Callihoo wearing Treaty Medal, inset, given to Chief Michel Callihoo
photo Ana Anubis, courtesy Musée Héritage Museum (#986.62.01)

fortunate that most people already had some livestock of their own because the animals didn't arrive until 1883.[23v] The Michel Reserve share was approximately 20 cows and 21 other cattle.[26] According to Treaty #6, they were entitled to some pigs as well.

Band members were eventually given farming equipment in the form of scythes, sickles, harrows, ploughs, hay forks, hay knives, reaping hooks, grain choppers and cradles. There were also tools such as saw files, grindstones, hoes, hand saws, augers, tool chests, pickaxes, frows, pit saws, spades and axes. Wagons, harness, trace chains and whiffletrees (part of the apparatus for hitching harness) were supplied. Each band was to receive seed for oats, wheat, barley and potatoes. The *Edmonton Bulletin* of June 10, 1882, reported that the Michel Reserve had 80 acres planted in crops.

Their first Treaty payment was described briefly in the *Saskatchewan Herald* of October 7, 1878. It reported that on October 4, in Edmonton, Indians including Iroquois from Jasper House, as well as Stonys and Crees, all received their annuities at Edmonton. From then on, in the late fall each year, government officials went to each reserve with the money for the annual payment. A North West Mounted Police officer handed out the cash to each member of the band. It was quite a formal occasion and was attended by the clergy. Merchants, especially from the Hudson's Bay Company, were out in force selling things and trying to collect their debts. In this first year they sold $2000 worth of goods.

An Order in Council was passed on May 17, 1889, PC 1151 confirming Michel Reserve #132.[51] Presentations of silver Treaty medals were not made until 1901, when the Duke and Duchess of Cornwall distributed them on behalf of the Crown, in Calgary. On this occasion the chiefs also received another medal commemorating the royal visit.

Reserve Life

The farmers on the Reserve must have put in a great deal of work in those first few years, for in the fall of 1884, the Inspector of Agencies says, "One can hardly realize that he is driving through an Indian Reserve. The large fields of grain, the strong straight fences, and good log houses in a country of mixed woods and prairie almost makes one fancy that he is driving through one of the newly settled districts of Ontario."[23 vi] This year, the crops had escaped hail and frost but the people hadn't planted enough potatoes for their needs. The Agent suggested giving out more seed but he had to wait for a reply from his boss before doing anything. There were two perennial problems. One was, of course, the unforgiving Alberta climate, its short growing season and risk of frost and hail. The other was the requirement to wait for decisions and arrangements to be made by the Department of Indian Affairs.

At legal maturity, each young man received a quarter section of land to use. His sisters were not entitled to any. Outsiders could become members of the band by marriage. If a woman was granted a discharge from Treaty, she received a lump sum which depended on the status of the trust account at the time.

As the years went by, more and more people wanted to be discharged from Treaty. Many members of Michel's Band obtained their discharge in 1885, paying back annuities received and applying for and receiving scrip. Some people who took scrip thought that the remaining members of the immediate family could still receive Treaty payments every year. They were in for quite a surprise! Other people believed that there would

---

After Michel's death, the medals were probably inherited by his wife, Philomène, and they then passed to the eldest daughter, Marie, who lived with her mother. They ended up in the hands of Michel's grandson, Patrick, who later told his wife, Jessie, that he wanted the museum in St. Albert to have them. Chief Michel's two medals are now in the collection of the Musée Héritage Museum in St. Albert.

There was also one continuing territorial dispute. The Agent remarked that a half-breed named L'Hirondelle encroached on the Reserve, and had built his house very near the line; he could not be persuaded to give up possession. Years and years of hassle ensued over the 40.9 acres that the young Janvier L'Hirondelle had occupied before the official survey and which was partly in the Reserve. He had applied for scrip and a scrip grant for his quarter section. There were attempts to resolve the issue over the years but after some irregularities in the surrender forms, the government having lost the documents, both sides were dug in. It turns out that Narcisse Beaudry first had the land, even before Treaty, and got Janvier L'Hirondelle to plough about four acres. While it was being surveyed, Beaudry, E. Brosseau, and Majeau came out and warned L'Hirondelle that the Surveyor had said to keep the line, because the Indians got to choose the land. Janvier was told not to do any more work. Then because Beaudry didn't pay L'Hirondelle for his work, the latter felt entitled to the land.

be a new scrip subscription for each generation, every twenty years or so. A report from an Agent in 1886 described the trouble they were having on other reserves. Many Indians of the Enoch Reserve also wanted their discharge in order to get scrip! Most were refused because they could not prove they were half-breeds and because the philosophy of Indian Affairs was that Native people had to be controlled, contained, and that they needed looking after as well.

Chief Michel collaborated with other local chiefs from time to time. The *Edmonton Bulletin* of March 28, 1881, says that the chiefs of the Alexander and Alexis Reserves met in council with Chief Michel. According to the paper, they also smoked a ceremonial pipe before adjournment.

Eighteen eighty-five was the year of the last Métis 'Rebellion'. During this period some Indian bands in the Edmonton region had rioted and made trouble. As Michel's Band was not one of these, the government distributed some cattle as rewards for loyalty to several people in the Band.[27]

It seems that most people either did not enjoy or could not afford to lead sedentary lives. According to the Indian Agent, Count de Caze, everyone was away from the Reserve in June and again in November and December, some people were off hunting. Inspector of Agencies T.P. Wadsworth remarked to Dewdney in 1887, however, that the Indians of

---

When in 1899 Gibbons, the Indian Agent, proposed that the band surrender the property because the claim predated the survey, the band rejected the idea. In 1903, Chief Michel and band were still unanimously opposed to ceding the land to L'Hirondelle's estate and said that they had earlier signed a surrender only under threats of deprivation of rations and withdrawal of government favour. By this time the place was let to a "Frenchman". Gibbons suggested a payment to the L'Hirondelle boys and provision of schooling for the girls. He also said that the land could be paid for but the Band did not want unknown strangers living there. Had these people become withdrawn, narrow-minded, even paranoid? It wouldn't be surprising, because in the end, the government transferred the disputed 40.92 acres to the estate of L'Hirondelle without official surrender by the band, and only Adolphus Callihoo got $9.00 for "improvements", that is, he had ploughed three acres. (Adolphus was Chief Michel's nephew and a member of the band.) Then there was a letter saying that taking money for this work meant agreeing to the claim! So he gave the money back but the Department said it never received it. Next there was an order that Indian Affairs release the land to the Department of the Interior. The L'Hirondelle estate did not get the land in the end, as the Minister, Frank Oliver, said it was only leased. Meanwhile Adolphus kept building on the land and finally signed a quit claim for $100 in 1912.[23 vii]

Michel's Band had cleared large fields. He also said that they kept horses and that freighting jobs should have been given them instead of to settlers.[23 xi] His report for 1888 compared two years on Michel's Reserve.[23 viii] The same acreage was under cultivation even though there were fewer potatoes planted, again because of shortage of seed. He said the Indians left upon this Reserve were in very comfortable circumstances and that it was impossible to deny them rations under the existing state of affairs, by which he meant a shortage of food. By the way, these relief rations included staples such as flour and beef, as well as tea, rice and tobacco.

Some trapping for fur animals continued on the Reserve into the next century. However, timber was its most important natural resource as a source of income. In some cases the rights to cut were sold. At other times, added value was achieved by cutting and hauling logs to a sawmill. In any case, because there was only a meagre living to be had on the Reserve, many men found outside work. The Hudson's Bay Company still employed people to transport goods on the rivers thus, many men took up freighting and were away for long periods, sometimes leaving their families poorly provided for. Women milked cows, made butter and sold what they could, often travelling for miles on foot lugging their produce, if they hadn't the use of a horse.

Hard Times

The year that frost destroyed most of the crops, 1887, was followed by a year of universal relief. The *Bulletin* of 1888 printed an article by Cunningham saying that the Indians at Lac La Biche and elsewhere were starving.[23 ix] Even the Michel Band had to be "rationed regularly".[23 x] By March, the Agent, a Major de Balinhard, complained that everyone is depending on the government for a living. That year there was also an excess of deaths over births in the Edmonton Region Indian Reserves, mainly due to an epidemic of measles. Hunger no doubt exacerbated the effects of the disease.

During this period of want, the Agent had tried to impress upon the Edmonton bands that they must do more for themselves. He had given them a small increase in rations but they were obliged to haul it from Edmonton themselves without getting paid for doing so. According to

Father Alexandre Blanchet, the priest at the Alexander Reserve, the Chiefs Alexander, Alexis, and Michel accompanied by two friends from St. Albert, Dan Maloney and John Cunningham, went to the Superintendent of the federal police to complain of their treatment over the winter. On the same day, February 23, 1888, they sent a telegram by CP Railway Telegraph to the Prime Minister, Sir John A. MacDonald, that said, "We are starving. We cannot get help from agency have killed some of the cattle on reserves to save our lives so far we don't want to kill any more but will have to unless we get help at once."[23x]

Chiefs Alexis, Alexander, and Michel also called on the *Edmonton Bulletin*, the same day, to make a statement that was printed on February 25, 1888.

> Alexander: "We have come here to make complaint that the government has not used us as they agreed. If they continue to use us during the rest of the winter up to the present time perhaps a few will see the spring but those who do will be too weak to do anything to help themselves. Before leaving we told a meeting at which the whole talk was to kill the government cattle or one of our own horses for food. It would be no use to kill the dogs for they were starving as well as us. We agreed that before we would die of starvation we would kill all the cattle. If the government will do anything for us we beg they will do so right away. We cannot stand the hunger any longer. If we do not get help at once we will have to kill the cattle the government has placed with us for our use, and we do not wish to do that as we know that would be our own loss. The government knows that other winters we were able to help ourselves killing fur which we could trade for food. With that and what the government then gave us we could live well enough. The government promised that in years of failure such as this they would help us more, but instead of doing so in this year of scarcity they have lessened the usual supply of food by more than one half."
>
> Michel: "If the government wishes us to live they must help us as quickly as possible. We see plainly that we cannot live on what they now give us and that we will die with it if they cannot do better. This winter we have no furs, no crop, no game, no fish. Last year I had 300 bushels of grain, this year not a bushel. Last year I had 100 bushels of potatoes, this year 15 bushels. We got a few fish from Lake St. Ann, but very few as the fishing there was a failure."
>
> Alexander remarked that they had half a crop of barley and that when they went fishing they did not catch enough to eat while doing so. Alexis also said that they had 125 bushels of grain the previous year and this year, none. Michel said that in other winters they used to get enough to live on from the government, about ten pounds of flour and five pounds of bacon per head every ten days. This year they got five pounds of flour every ten days and bacon occasionally.

The Agent telegraphed to his boss that there were tons of food at the agencies but the Indians wouldn't haul it unless they got paid for freighting! Finally Assistant Commissioner Haytor Reed came to see for himself. He visited the Alexander Reserve but his talks with Chief Alexander did not go well and the chief insisted on an official meeting to be held in Edmonton. Father Blanchet described this "public interview" that was held at the police barracks in Edmonton. The participants were the Chiefs, Michel and Alexander and their Councillors, Haytor Reed and Major de Balinhard of Indian Affairs, Superintendent Griesbach and Inspector Casey of the North West Mounted Police, Mr. Young of the Hudson's Bay Company, the Reverend Father Blanchet, Dan Maloney, John Rowland, interpreter, and Mr. Reed's own interpreter. There was an exchange of views but the outcome was not very satisfactory.[68 i]

Father Blanchet described the meeting:[68i]

"Mr. Reed said he had come in pursuance of his promise of the day before to hear what the Indians had to say.

Alexander said he spoke as it might be for God and for the government on behalf of the poor people who could not speak for themselves. 'I don't depend on what you are doing here—both of you (Messrs. Reed and de Balinhard). Everything has been going badly since you two came here. We consider that you have acted against the law. It is you who have caused the government cattle to be killed. You knew last fall the game and fish had failed in this country. You have come from far and you have seen no track of anything to kill and eat. You see how miserable the Indians are here, and when you go back you will tell them all is well.'

Mr. Reed – 'You told me all this when I spoke to you before, and I gave you your answer then. The government is pretty well aware of the facts of the case. My business here is to report the facts to the government which I will do.'

Alexander – 'What I say is truth, as everyone who is here knows. Because it is true I sent the telegram to Sir John. I have waited for an answer, but have got none. I am not as wise as you. I look like a dog before you, but I have a mind to think of these things. I follow the track of the law, and I am not ashamed. White men would do as we have done. We killed our cattle from hunger. Hunger might make us kill each other. It is you were pushing us to do evil. That we have eaten our horses and the cattle that the government gave us should be blamed on you. What the poor people are saying every day rings in my ears. We do not depend on you.'

Mr. Reed – 'Does he mean that the promises I made him yesterday won't be kept?'

Alexander – 'I am talking not of what is ahead, but of what is behind, since last fall.'

Michel – 'When we were forced with hunger we went to the agent here. He spoke well to us, but that did not fill us. When matters did not improve we said: Let us see how it is farther away. We got no answer from the telegram we sent. We see that nothing is going right from Regina. You knew that it was a hard year with us. If you wanted to save us why did you not send the food while the roads were good. The agent had asked for 500 sacks of flour this winter. He heard that only 300 sacks had been sent.'

Mr. Reed said that the total number of sacks of flour asked for was 500 but the government were using its judgement about the time of delivery.

Mr. de Balinhard said that was the trouble 200 were not to be delivered till June.

Rev. Father Blanchet, at Michel's request, conversed with Mr. Reed in French.

Oskenikiw (Joseph Gladu) blamed the Regina officials and accused them of misusing the money placed in the hands of the government for the benefit of the Indians. He said, 'You do not expend as much this year as before. When we could help ourselves you helped us more, this year we cannot help ourselves and you help us less.'

Mr. Reed – 'I am here on behalf of the government to see whether the Indians can provide for themselves or not. After making inquiries I find that they require more rations. Consequently I increased them and will allow them a reasonable quantity until such time as those who are able go off to hunt. The government does not wish anyone to suffer from lack of food. But though the government aids the Indians and in most cases very liberally, the Indians are expected to aid themselves by every means in their power. As I told you, my promises are being kept and both flour and meat are being sent out to you so that you will not want.'

Alexander – 'I understand that the government said, If you help yourselves we will help you not, if you help yourselves, we will leave you off. You know it is deep snow and a hard season. You knew these things before. If you had opened your eyes before, things would not be as they are. But you did not wish to see you want to do nothing but gather money. Your name is neither good with Indians or whites—neither of you '

Another councilor (Attikusis) – 'I am a coward, but when I hear my children cry from hunger, I kill cattle. I think of you as the cold you want to kill all on the reserves.'

Alexander - 'You were sent word last spring about sickness on the reserves. On my own Reserve many have died of sickness and hunger. Medicine is no use without food. Thirty have died on my own Reserve, and fifteen besides. Five of my children have died, most of them grown up. I sent word every day, but you would do nothing for me. You think what I say of the sickness is not true. I tell you in your ears, you lie when you say you take the part of sick children. Mr. Juin had been used to working for the whites. This winter he could get no work. There was no game and no fish, and he had nearly starved to death depending on the Indian Department. He did not go to the whites to sell his country. They came to him to buy it, and now they would not pay the price.'

Mr. Reed ordered dinner to be provided for the Indians, and answered them that they would receive the Increase of rations promised."

Father Blanchet then remarked "les sauvages ne sont pas satisfaits."[68i] [the Indians are not satisfied.]

The Agent states a different view of the whole affair in his report to Indian Affairs. De Balinhard said he promised the Indians an increase in relief and then they still would not haul it[23 ix]. He reports that rations are hard to obtain from the contractor, especially flour. He remarks that the people could have managed by going hunting. The people on reserves didn't like or trust this agent, who also believed that they would use extra rations to feed their non-Treaty relatives. He even held the opinion that men got more rations by starving the old women.[23 xx]

According to Father Blanchet, promises made by Haytor Reed still weren't kept and people continued to suffer from extreme hunger at Alexander. Chiefs Michel and Alexander wrote to the Minister, the Honourable Mister White, stating some demands. They wanted the agent removed, cattle to replace the ones they had to slaughter, and more rations. They also wanted a transfer of Roman Catholic band members from the Enoch Reserve to their own two reserves and a Roman Catholic industrial school built for all the children. A priest in Ottawa talked to the Prime Minister and wrote that he was led to believe these things would be forthcoming. However, not one of these demands was ever met. On the contrary, Balinhard brought the police to Alexander Reserve to enforce payment to the government for the cattle they had been obliged to kill. Father Blanchet went on to say that this Agent would not even give the doctor the money required for medical supplies to treat the Indians.[68 i]

Later in 1888, rations were doled out once a month, although the crops had started to do better. The Michel Band began to do the freighting to Lac Ste-Anne for the government agency as the people there couldn't do it for themselves. Michel no longer used oxen, but ponies for this job; however, they still employed oxen as draft animals at Alexander Reserve as late as 1894.[27] These freighters were paid 25% less than the usual commercial rate because of the rations and other advantages they got from the government. The Agent still described the Michel people as "comfortable and contented".

There were many contagious diseases around at the end of the nineteenth century, including diphtheria, measles, scarlet fever and tuberculosis, as well as the dreaded smallpox. Michel's band escaped much of the consumption and measles. The other bands in the region were so afflicted that the men couldn't even hunt, forcing the Agent to provide them with food. The government doctor, Dr. Wilson, was sent to treat the sick and he also vaccinated everyone against smallpox. Unfortunately there were no shots as yet for measles. The Callihoo children at the industrial school near High River were also vaccinated in the late 1880s.[68 vi] They had the good fortune of having an attentive doctor there. There was an epidemic of smallpox in 1891, and again the government came through with vaccinations for the people on reserves and students at the school.

Life Goes On

Any farmer will tell you that it is not possible to run a successful operation without appropriate equipment and machinery. The Michel Reserve got into big trouble with the government because, without authority from Indian Affairs, they traded seven steers to a settler for a mowing machine, rake and three wagons. This insubordination was reported on July 1, 1889. They couldn't borrow equipment from Chief Michel because he put up a hundred tons of hay each year which kept his own mower fully occupied, besides which, he lived nine miles from anyone else. The 'culprits' argued that they believed that as they had raised the steers, they could dispose of them. The government first asserted that the original twenty cows were "presents" as defined in the Indian Act, that is, obtained at government expense. The band wanted a court decision. Vankoughnet of Indian Affairs finally said these were not presents and that trading them was only a crime if it was done by individuals without common consent.[86] We don't know how the matter was resolved but it shows the kind of thing that the band was up against. This may help account for the continuing drift of band members from the Reserve.

In his report of 1890, de Caze said there were 95 souls on the Reserve.[23 xiii] McGibbon, in his 1891 report, said there were only 37 people on the Reserve.[23 xiii] Accordingly, there must have been a number who lived there but were not paid an annuity. By this time there were only six heads of families who were band members actually living there. There were seventeen houses, some empty, and twenty-two stables.

Michel and some band members came to see de Caze at the agency at Stony Plain. They still needed ploughs and harrows. De Caze reported that he told them as he told the other bands, that he had none. He added that the people were willing to work but did not have the necessary implements. De Caze recommended ten breaking ploughs, two cross ploughs and five harrows be given to each Reserve and suggests that the cost (about 600 dollars) be taken out of the flour and meat rations for twelve days.[23 xiii] It is obvious that they might not have needed so many rations if they had been able to buy the tools needed to farm properly!

Department of Indian Affairs Inspector, McGibbon described the people on the Reserve, in 1891,[23 xix] as "well-to-do", with nice homes and outbuildings including pig houses, hen houses and milk houses. There were good fences and fine new stables and the buildings were very well looked after. The houses were whitewashed with white clay, outside and in. They had box and cooking stoves, bedsteads, tables and other furniture. The Chief's brother had added a wing to his house and another man was building a new and better house for himself. McGibbon said that some clothing was still made of animal hides. He went on to remark that these women made shirts from flour sacks and said the children were well clad, neat and clean. One might suppose they were—in their flour sacks. But how well-to-do were they?

At this time, the Inspector reported that they had nineteen acres in wheat, six acres in oats, thirty in barley, two acres in potatoes and an acre of gardens. The Band had a herd of seven oxen, two bulls, twelve cows, four steers, two heifers, three bull calves, three heifer calves and twelve pigs in addition to the sixteen horses, seven cows, fifteen young cattle, and twelve pigs that were in private hands. They made their own hay racks, bob sleds, fork handles and some harness. They also made butter.[23 xix] All this was in apparent contrast to the situation on other reserves.[23 xiv]

The Department of Indian Affairs did try various means of improving the economic lot of the Indians. The *Edmonton Bulletin* reported in March 1887, that the Department planned to plant wild rice, experimentally, in the next season. It granted $1500 toward a grist mill in St. Albert with the proviso that Indian work had precedence two days a week and that Indians be tolled or charged for no more than six bushels of grain.[27] This mill was built in 1889. Agent de Caze was quite a gardener and seemed full of optimism in 1891. He grew thousands of young cabbage plants and gave them to the Indians and he was growing ash and maple trees for them to put around their houses. He had also grown hemp successfully for making rope to mend harness and for tying bags. He planned to try peas, buckwheat and flax. A Hereford bull was brought from Calgary to improve the quality of the Reserve herds.

In some instances, repression and paternalism by the Indian Agent went rather far. During a period when there was very little available to eat, some people on the Alexander Reserve again killed a heifer. The Indian Agent, Count de Caze, wrote in his 1892 report that he had cut their rations off, apparently as a punishment. That was also the year that the police were called in to search the reserves for liquor. The chiefs and headmen on some other reserves in the Edmonton Region were in trouble for drunkenness. De Caze noted at the same time that everything was in order on the Michel Reserve.[23 xv]

The Michel Reserve maintained its excellent reputation with the Department of Indian Affairs. A memorandum states, "... the homesteads compare very favourably with those of any White settlers. The houses are of a superior kind and well furnished. The stables and corrals are all substantial and well put up. Livestock is good and the Indians are well equipped with implements. ... These Indians are industrious and law abiding and far advanced in farming and civilization generally."[62]

The band still needed machinery and implements. Michel 'Coliou' and twelve other defendants were taken to court because they owed about $300 on machinery bought between 1900 and 1903.[84] These included a grain crusher, a separator and bagger and a steam grain crusher.

In 1903, the band requested that they be put on the "independence list" to manage their own affairs which meant that they would be able to sell grain and cattle without reference to the department and they would undertake to ask nothing henceforth from the Indian Affairs either. The request was apparently denied.[22 xxii] It wasn't until around 1915 that an amendment to the Indian Act was passed, allowing the disposal of livestock without permission.[23 iii]

Surrender of Land

A document surrendering seven square miles of land along the western limit of the Reserve was signed on July 20, 1903, in order to raise money for about $13,000 worth of badly needed farm equipment.[23 xvi] The men who signed were Michel Callihoo, his son Albert and his daughter's husband Pierre Jean Berland. Joseph Gladu, Jean Baptiste Callihoo and his sons, Louis Jerome, Timothy and Sévère also signed. Then Michel and James Gibbons, the Indian Agent appeared before the Acting Deputy Registrar General of Canada on 18 August, 1903, and swore that there had been majority assent from adult male members of the Band, that there had been a proper meeting of the Band Council, that all who voted were entitled to do so, and that Michel was the Chief. This surrender was effected by Order in Council #1545 on Sept. 15, 1903.

They needed binders, ploughs, and seed drills. They needed horses, too. They also required a threshing outfit with engine and a sawmill planer and matcher.[23 xvii] The Agent, Gibbons, was keen on the surrender although there might have been alternative ways to obtain the money needed. For instance, they could have cut and sold some lumber themselves as the surrendered land had the most valuable timber on the Reserve.[86] The Commissioner for the Department of Indian Affairs, Laird, wrote a patronizing letter saying they shouldn't get the implements because, in his opinion, Indians were uniformly feckless and careless. He thought the crop didn't warrant a thresher and that the sawmill equipment was "premature".

In spite of these disagreements, the Department finally agreed that stock and implements would be purchased from the proceeds of the sale. The land was thus put up for sale in the winter of 1903–04. However, in 1904, the Department denied the band's request for an advance on the profits so that they might buy some nine horses for spring work. Michel joined the other chiefs in petitioning the Department to remove Agent Gibbons.

A small number of ads for the sale of the land had been placed in the newspapers that included the *Toronto Globe, Manitoba Free Press, Edmonton Bulletin*, and *Alberta German Herald*, and additional notices were sent to some people in Manitoba and elsewhere who had shown some interest in another reserve sale. The result was that very few tenders came in and most of these were from Ontario. The land was valued at

Plate 15. Timothy Callihoo, standing. Seated man may be his older brother, Chief Louis Jerome Callihoo ca. 1898
photo Ernest Brown, *Provincial Archives of Alberta*

$4.28 per acre and sold on average for $3.08 per acre. Some parcels brought less than $2.00 an acre. Chief Michel was so concerned that he wrote to the Department of Indian Affairs, saying, "We send you these few lines to let you know that we would not like to let our strip of land go for less than $3.00 an acre, for $1.50 is too low. We would not be able to work. We beg of you to send over a gentleman to visit our agency to settle everything right."[30] Nearly eighty per cent of the land actually remained unsold. The largest purchaser (about 25% of the total available) was a lady who was employed as a cleaner in Indian Affairs offices earning $5.00 per month. Only some of the principal due was paid some years later and in 1908, she assigned two of her three quarter sections to an Indian Affairs clerk. There were other peculiar purchases as well. The unsold land was then kept off the market even though there was some interest in it.[86]

Another surrender was requested in October 1905, to provide the Villeneuve settlers with the strip on the eastern end of the Reserve to round off their properties. The band refused as they were still waiting for some benefit from the previous surrender. Soon afterwards, Mr. Frank Oliver of Indian Affairs was informed that the previously surrendered land was now valued at only $3.84 an acre. Within days, the unsold land was traded at that exact price to a Claude Galinger of a company called Crafts and Lee Land and Business Exchange.[86]

There was also the issue of a fence along the eastern boundary that was apparently required to keep cattle owned by the settlers outside the Reserve from wandering onto Reserve land. The settlers didn't have to keep their cows in; rather, the Indians had to keep them out! The Inspector said the Department would pay for it if it were built of wood. Against these recommendations, the band decided to build a wire fence to reduce the risk of fire.

On January 4, 1906, the frustrated Michel Band wrote a letter offering to quit Treaty in exchange for clear title to one section of land per family and the sale of the surrendered area to be paid over in cash! Inspector Markle of the Department said that this idea would not be entertained.[86]

The Department kept chipping away at the real estate and the Michel Band kept trying to obtain money for the things they needed. The government wanted to build a road between the settlers and the Reserve on land which would have to be surrendered. Again the settlers weren't the ones who had to give up anything. The band agreed to a surrender of the eastern half sections provided that a farming outfit be provided for eight people consisting of eleven teams of horses, eleven sets of harness and eleven farm wagons. They also demanded that the land be sold for no less than $10.00 per acre and that they receive their equipment as soon as there are funds from the sale. Inspector Markle thought that the land in question for surrender was not in use but this was not so as four band members had made "improvements" here.[86] The majority of band members then started to have second thoughts about this surrender because they never saw any real benefits from previous sales.

It is clear from all this that the Department spent little on the Band, little or no money came into the Band account, and thus the members of the band couldn't get on with the business of farming or anything else! They finally did surrender the land, which was sold for about $28,500. Although this would have well covered the equipment, worth about $5000, needed by the band, they could only use ten percent according to a rule in the Indian Act.[86]

The Minister of the Interior, Frank Oliver, then introduced a bill in the House of Commons allowing up to 50% of the purchase price to go to the Indians. This made surrender a much more attractive proposition and so more property was finally put up for sale. However, there seems to have been some skullduggery here. Ultimately two speculators (one was Mr. Oliver's son-in-law) bought 75% of the land but of the some $50,000 which the Department should have received, only about two percent was paid by January 1910, and none by these two buyers. Payments were only made after the property was assigned to another speculator who paid less than the original value. In future years great profits were made out of this excellent real estate. Mineral rights for most of the property remained in the hands of the Crown, however. Of all the people who profited, one of the main ones was Frank Oliver who ended up with 3,400 acres of the former Michel Reserve, comprising 26 of the 60 parcels sold in 1906.[51]

The government arbitrarily settled the L'Hirondelle dispute (described above) by making a free grant of the disputed 40.92 acres to the L'Hirondelle family in 1911, by Order in Council P.C. 2717 without the band's consent on the grounds that the Crown had the right to deal with settlers in any way it saw fit.[51]

There were a number of other surrenders of land. For instance, the Canadian Northern Railway obtained expropriated land through the north end for the railroad in 1910. In 1918, the Band agreed to surrender a narrow strip of land that got sold to adjacent land owners and there was land given up at different times for road allowances.[51]

Religion and Education

Everyone on the Reserve was a Roman Catholic. Most were baptized, married, and moreover were buried at Lac Ste-Anne, St. Albert or Villeneuve. A priest made the rounds at intervals. For instance, Father Grandin left St. Albert to visit the reserves on December 29, 1885. Chief Michel donated logs from the Reserve to construct the church of St. Peter at Villeneuve. Eighteen Reserve families attended church here regularly. Those who were more comfortable in the Cree language, such as Albert Callihoo's wife, Marguerite, would go to the church at Rivière-Qui-Barre (Alexander Reserve) while some families preferred to go to the old log church at Winterburn.

Each year, from its inception in 1889, Native people would make the pilgrimage to Lac Ste-Anne whose waters had the reputation of healing. The families of the Reserve were no exception. Among the first pilgrims in that June were Michel's sister-in-law Angelique, his son Louis and his nephew Timothy. The following July, Michel's wife Philomene, his brother Jean Baptiste and his sisters Cécile and Angelique were there.[68v] This required a long trip by wagon or buggy, but it was not to be missed! John Cunningham, a grandson of the original John Cunningham of St. Albert, made the trip on foot three times! You would stop for the night. One example of a stopping place was Dog Creek, and you could then make it to the campsite at the Mission the following day. The horses were pastured, the tents put up and then serious visiting could begin. Some people camped there for the whole week. There were numerous Masses, special blessings for the sick, and Stations of the Cross. Everyone dipped into the lake at least once.

The first school was built on the Reserve in 1949, which was rather late for three generations of people. This was not because there was no interest in having the children educated. It was so urgent that there had been talk in 1889 of members of other reserves, such as Enoch joining Michel's Reserve and occupying the "empty farms", making a more powerful group to demand a school as promised in the Treaty. The school was open for only about six years after which the students were taken by bus to Villeneuve or St. Albert.

However, there was an industrial school at High River, east of Okotoks, built in 1884 for the Plains Nations' children. Most of the parents of these children, however, refused to bring their children to the school and the few older kids who attended often ran away. That was why Father Lacombe, the first Principal, had the idea of bringing sixteen 'Cree' children to the school in November of 1885. The majority were from Michel's band but there were also children from Enoch's and Papasschew's Reserves.

At least the students learned something at this school near Dunbow. Experts taught the students valuable trades, including the mechanics and operation of steam engines. They had to put in a half day of field work, carpentry, shoemaking, and cleaning known as "fatigue", and of course the girls learned embroidery and knitting and so on. They also did their own laundry (even the boys). Almost all the children at the school were Native, so that there was less opportunity for discrimination against them in favour of settlers' kids. At first the children were taken south to the school by their parents in wagons; and later they travelled by coach and train.

Some students were sent to the Grey Nuns Convent in St. Albert for their education in this period. Father Blanchet had a poor opinion of this school. He was hoping to open an industrial school at Alexander for the students from Alexander's and Michel's Reserves and described the convent in St. Albert, scathingly, "qui passe pour une école industrielle"[68 i] [which passes for an industrial school]. After Dunbow closed in 1922, the Convent provided the only schooling available to Reserve children unless they could live with relatives and go to a public school in a town. In 1898, one of the Callihoo girls, either Isabelle or Christina, conducted lessons on the Reserve for young children and also taught the boys and girls to knit and sew.[27]

Plate 16. Annual Pilgrimage to Lac Ste-Anne, n.d.
Provincial Archives of Alberta

Lifestyles

Although, as in Louis' time, people travelled by boat, horseback, and occasional dog teams, most had a horse and wagon, or they might own a carriage called a Democrat. In the early days some trees were big enough to scoop out for dugout boats. Louis Jerome used one to get downriver to St. Albert. Some few people bought cars in the 1920s—Vital Victor Callihoo had the first one on the reserve. Sam Callihoo had a Model A Ford which he drove to the Lac Ste-Anne pilgrimage. However, many, including his mother, still used their horses which were more suited to the roads! You can imagine what the rutted dirt roads would have been like in the spring. If a medical emergency occurred or a fire broke out, it was really difficult to get help from outside.

As the shops were rather far away, itinerant peddlers were welcome. Anne Anderson says that in the 1930s there were 'Jews or Syrians' who carried bolts of cloth and sewing supplies. There were also sausage peddlers who came to the Reserve. Hector Hebert came by with hamburger and sausage but always stayed on the road. Another man sold Rawley's patent medicines. Like everyone else in Canada, the people of the Reserve ordered all manner of things from Eaton's Catalogue.

There wasn't much time for fun as there was so much work to do around the house and farm. However, fishing was a family diversion on weekends. Berry picking was also a family activity in the late summer. Kids played baseball and hockey. The Church put on social events and some people liked to have card parties. When there was a dance, a wagon drawn by horses came to round people up. The driver of the wagon had to know where each young lady lived along the way! There were excellent musicians in the family who played for traditional Métis dances as well as the more fashionable dances of the day.

Technology at the Reserve remained old-fashioned to the end. They never did get running water, electricity or telephones. Laundry was done with river water: you had to take the team or truck down to the river and bring the water back in barrels. Drinking water was pumped up by hand from a well. Before drilling a well, you had to locate underground water by "dowsing" with a forked stick. In the hands of certain people, such as Mary Callihoo, the pointed end would turn down where there was water.

Potatoes and turnips could be stored in a root cellar and some people had real ice houses where they kept ice blocks cut from the river. Victor and Clothilde Callihoo hung their meat and cream in the well to keep it cold and fresh. Like many other rural folk they baked their own bread, made clothes and blankets, and many tools were manufactured from something else. Of course, they had to know how to do their own repairs on machinery.

Some people cut the timber on the Reserve for profit. Others who lived near the road sold it at fifty cents a load in the 1930s to such people as Henry Belcourt, who was a great-grandnephew of Chief Michel. The wood could be sold for three dollars a cord delivered in Edmonton. Parts of the property were sometimes rented. For example, Tobie Hodgson, an in-law from St. Albert, lived on the Reserve with his family for eight years.

Aboriginal skills were retained here until well into the twentieth century. Instead of bed springs, there were boughs cut from trees. Mattresses were sometimes made of feathers and soft, light, warm blankets were made of rabbit skins cut in strips. These were twisted and then fastened into a flannel cover and washable sheets placed over the whole thing. These are the sorts of things that people like to remember with nostalgia about their parents' lifestyle.

Building paper was put on the inside walls of the house and then covered with calcimine (a kind of whitewash). The paper was removed and changed each year so that the mice and bugs could be cleaned out. Floors were plain wood and the girls of the family had to scrub them with a brush until they were nearly white. On the wall in every home hung a crucifix. Many women also hung an attractive bag embroidered with bead work to store matches and other small things. Old-fashioned herbal remedies were used for healing.

A few branches of the Callihoo family have a rare genetic makeup. Some individuals have a chromosomal deficiency that can result in incompatibility between mother and fetus and thus, miscarriage. This was discovered and studied by physicians for the Red Cross in 1954.[8] A number of generous members of the family donated blood to the Red Cross when it was needed for a patient in California who had the same rare condition. The medical people had to go by truck to the Reserve, obtain the blood, and rush it back to Edmonton whence it was shipped to the U.S. by the Canadian Air Force.

Politics

Joseph Gladu, the headman of the Michel Band, died in 1906. On April 20, 1910, the Indian Agent told the Department that the Michel Band had requested a Councillor be appointed to look after the Reserve because the chief was too sick to perform any of his duties. A year later, there was another letter informing the Department that old Chief Michel Callihoo of the Michel Reserve died on the eighth of April at his home. The agent was instructed to appoint one councillor and to have the band choose only a new chief. The people stomped out of a meeting held at Treaty time because they couldn't agree. The agent didn't wish to open the matter again right away. Finally the band elected Louis Jerome, Michel's nephew, as Chief, and Solomon, Michel's son, as Headman for an indefinite term.[23 xviii] Louis Jerome was Chief for only four years. Solomon succeeded him, in 1917, as Chief for the next eighteen years.

In 1928, ten Callihoo families voluntarily decided to give up their Indian status. This is called enfranchisement, because the rights and obligations of ordinary citizenship are assumed, including the right to vote. They comprised 41 of the 130 people who received an annuity in 1927. Those who signed the document were Adolphus, William, Henry, Vital Victor, and Louis Jerome's widow, Victoria. James, three of his sons and Albert's son, Isidor, also signed the document. The Order in Council, P.C. 35/811 of May 15, 1928, gave each member of these families its share of band funds. Out of this money, each would then be allowed to buy a part of the Reserve of a magnitude proportionate to the size of the family. The price was fixed by the Department at $6 per acre. Patents were issued for 2,892 acres. Although these lands were now no longer Reserve lands, mineral rights stayed with the land.[50] The move was probably made so that this group of people could have the freedom to prosper from their work. Unfortunately, not all of these men made wise choices for their futures and got into financial difficulties. It was too late to go back to the relative security of the Reserve. Many of the Callihoos, however, became active, contributing members of the community of Spruce Grove. Within a year, James had already given some of his property to build the Michael School and Vital Victor served as a Spruce Grove School Trustee. The children of these families must have been happy to attend public school instead of having to leave home to be educated. On November 13, 1993, there was a reunion of students who attended this school.

Hugh Dempsey, the historian, says that the Band tried in 1931 and again in 1949 to achieve freedom from government control and be enfranchised. Later, in the early 1950s, Johnny Callihoo participated in a meeting where he insisted that a proposed Indian Act Bill 267 retain a clause that permitted an entire reserve to enfranchise.[22]

Fred Callihoo, a grandson of Jean Baptiste, was elected Chief from 1936 until 1948. He was succeeded by Michel's grandson, Roderick Callihoo, until 1958. From 1949 to 1954, Johnny Rodgers was his Headman. Michel's son Solomon had the post of Headman from 1954 to 1957 and Sam Callihoo, Michel's grandson, was Headman at the end, in 1958.

Who was Chief from 1955 to 1958? Transcripts from the account book for Triennial Clothing under Treaty Provisions show that it was Roderick Callihoo who ordered and received his suits of clothing as Chief in those years. Headmen Johnny Rodgers, Solomon Callihoo, and Sam Callihoo also received their triennial clothing at various times between 1949 and 1958.

The entire band was enfranchised thirty years later, on 31 March, 1958 by Order in Council P.C. 375.

Occupied land was to be deeded to the occupiers if they were eligible. There was a plan put forward which provided for division of funds and disposal of lands. The plan also stated that the Government of Canada would continue to assume the cost of relief and education for twelve months for eligible band members. The Governor General in Council pursuant to subsection 1 of Section 111 of the Indian Act approved the plan at a meeting on March 18, 1958.

The Reserve was divided up in the following fashion. 7,509 acres were granted by individual patents to Band families and individuals. This left 2,160 acres to be sold at auction which was held at St. Albert on June 9, 1958.[50] Road allowances were transferred without charge to the Province

Under "comments", government policy is revealed to the effect that vouchers up to the value of $78 for a business suit or coded cheques are available if a made-to-measure uniform is not desired.

of Alberta. After all outstanding accounts were dealt with, the balance was to be distributed on a *per capita* basis among the members of the band with Trust provisions for minors. The total amount expected to be paid out was around $100,000. Eligible band members were numerous Callihoos, Brelands, Rodgers and a Courtereille (some 121 people in all).

Not everyone was happy about this. According to Beatrice Callihoo, her father Solomon believed that Chief Michel's trust and legacy were being destroyed. The government had ruled that everyone must vote on the issue, even women, and Solomon thought that it was their vote that was the deciding factor.

In the 1928 enfranchisement, the mineral rights were deeded along with the land. In this instance a company called Michel Investments was incorporated in 1958 to hold in trust 1276.5 acres containing gravel deposits. All the mineral rights underlying the 10,946 acres of the Reserve and some of the road allowances were also patented to the company.[50] So far, except for a brief period when there was an unsuccessful gas well, this property has produced only gravel.

Each legitimate member of the Band was to receive an equal number of shares in the company and these shareholders were to be given priority on the purchase of shares offered for sale. A member was defined as someone who was on the Membership Roll at the date of enfranchisement, the estate of registered band members who died on or after July 1, 1956, and any person who is shown before the distribution of moneys to be entitled to be registered. The sale moneys that should have been deposited with Michel Investments Ltd. were around $53,000.[51] There are people, now, who believe they have legitimate claims but have not yet been able to establish them.

Since Bill C-31, about 500 descendants of people in the original Michel Band have regained Indian status. They have formed an association with an elected Council and Chief; the present chief is Gilbert Anderson, a great grandson of Chief Michel. The new Michel Band has petitioned the Federal

At the insistence of Solomon those members who were incapable of looking after themselves, some nine people or so, were to be placed on the General List, thus retaining their status, so that the government would still look after them.

Government "to resume recognition and services to the Michel Band on the same basis as services and recognition are provided to other Bands/ Indian Nations in Canada". In November 1989, a presentation was also made to the National Aboriginal Inquiry on the Impact of Bill C-31. The presentation recommended that "the Federal Government immediately re-establish formal recognition to the Michel Band and that serious negotiations for a Michel Band land base begin simultaneously." Negotiations with the Federal Government are still going on.

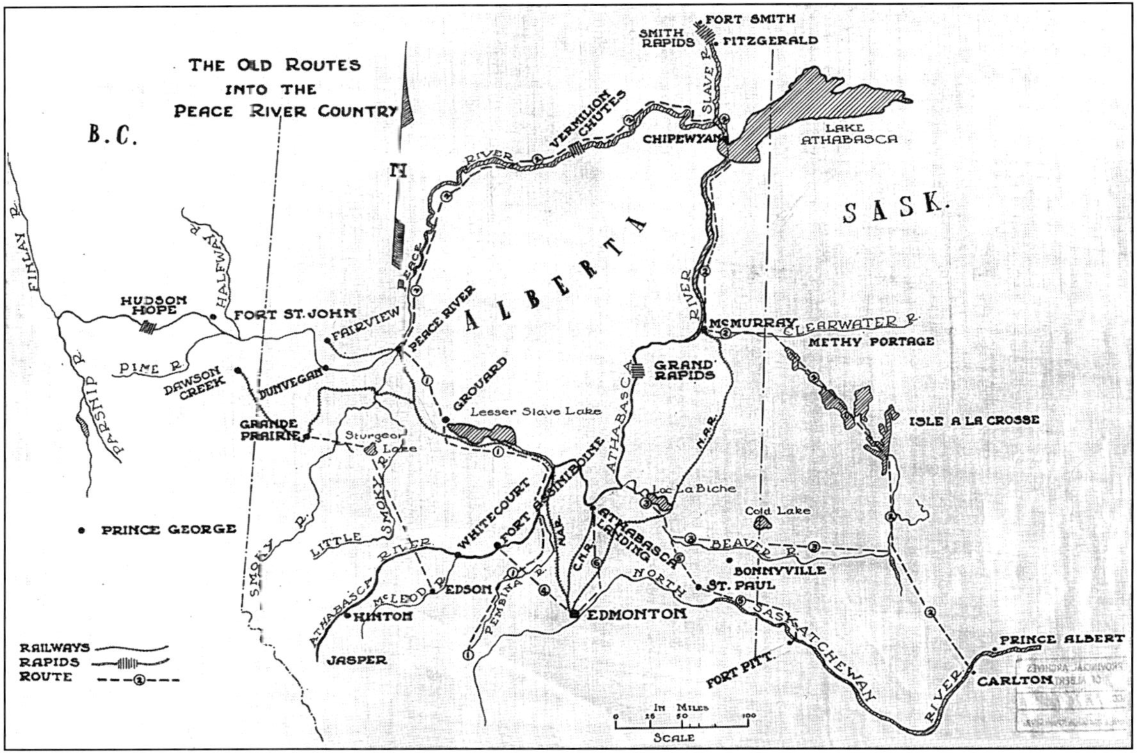
THE OLD ROUTES
INTO THE
PEACE RIVER COUNTRY
B.C.
ALBERTA
SASK.
FORT SMITH
SMITH RAPIDS
FITZGERALD
SLAVE R.
VERMILION CHUTES
CHIPEWYAN
LAKE ATHABASCA
RIVER
PEACE
FINLAY R.
HALFWAY R.
HUDSON HOPE
FORT ST. JOHN
FAIRVIEW
PEACE RIVER
PINE R.
DAWSON CREEK
DUNVEGAN
PARSNIP R.
GROUARD
Lesser Slave Lake
GRANDE PRAIRIE
Sturgeon Lake
PRINCE GEORGE
SMOKY R.
LITTLE SMOKY R.
WHITECOURT
FORT ASSINIBOINE
ATHABASCA RIVER
McLEOD R.
EDSON
HINTON
JASPER
PEMBINA R.
N.A.R.
C.N.R.
ATHABASCA LANDING
EDMONTON
McMURRAY
CLEARWATER R.
METHY PORTAGE
GRAND RAPIDS
ATHABASCA
N.A.R.
ISLE A LA CROSSE
Lac La Biche
Cold Lake
BEAVER R.
BONNYVILLE
ST. PAUL
NORTH SASKATCHEWAN RIVER
FORT PITT
PRINCE ALBERT
CARLTON
RAILWAYS
RAPIDS
ROUTE
IN MILES
0 25 50 100
SCALE

Plate 17. Map, hand-drawn, 1952
Provincial Archives of Alberta (79.269/63d)

THE LIVES AND TIMES OF SOME LATER GENERATIONS

The third and subsequent generations of Callihoos have taken various routes from their freeman origins to join in the mainstream of society. Many other members of the family also played a recorded part in the story of Alberta in the past hundred years. Although some people spread out from this region, many remained not far from the Edmonton/St. Albert area. The lives of the chiefs of the Michel Reserve are used here as specific examples of their times and described in some detail. The second Chief, Louis Jerome, succeeded his uncle Michel as Chief of the Michel Band in 1911, but remained in the position only until 1915 when he decided to move away from the Reserve.

Louis Jerome and Victoria Callihoo

Louis Jerome was the second son of Jean Baptiste Calliou and Angélique Bruneau. One grandfather was the Iroquois voyageur Louis Callihoo and the other may have been a son of the Baptiste Bruneau who travelled with David Thompson. One grandmother was Métis and the other's identity is still a mystery. Louis Jerome was born in 1858 while his dad was employed at Fort Edmonton and where they probably lived for a year or so. The family then moved to Lac Ste-Anne where Louis spent his childhood. He had two brothers close in age to play with and nine younger sisters and brothers. There were also lots of cousins. Here at Lac Ste-Anne, his father and uncle Michel ran a fishery where he no doubt had to work.

When Louis Jerome was twenty, he married the 'girl next door', seventeen-year-old Victoria Belcourt. Her parents were Alexis Belcourt and Nancy Rowand. Her paternal granddad, Joseph Belcourt, was another voyageur from Eastern Canada, married to Catherine L'Hirondelle, the daughter of an old Northwest Company voyageur, while her maternal grandmother was Archange Nipissing, married to Antoine Rowand, a son of a Chief Factor at Fort Edmonton. Like Louis, Victoria came from a family of about a dozen kids. It is she who has given us much insight about life at Lac Ste-Anne in a number of published interviews.

Lac Ste-Anne's main virtue for those who lived there was that there was a tremendous quantity of whitefish in the lake. Father de Smet said there were 70,000 pounds of whitefish caught there in 1846.[79] Father Lacombe said that without fish the poor people who lived off the land would die of starvation. According to him 50,000 fish were caught with nets in fifteen days.[44]

Changes

The young couple and their small children moved from Lac Ste-Anne to the Michel Reserve around 1880. Shortly afterward, Victoria suffered the loss of her father by misadventure. Her dad and mum went fishing on Lac Ste-Anne at the end of October and unfortunately broke through the ice. Mrs. Belcourt survived by clinging to a longitudinal pole for two hours until help came, but Alexis, with his arms spread on the ice, couldn't hang on that long and finally perished in only six to eight feet of water.[27]

Jean Baptiste had the following children with his wife, Angélique Bruneau (183?–?): Jean Felix (1855–1918) married Adèle Wanyandi then Eliza Omowaskew; Louis Jerome (1858–1926) married Victoria Anne Belcourt; John (1860–1890) married Olive L'Hirondelle; Angélique (1862–1905) married Jean L'Hirondelle; Justine (1864–?) married David Savard; Timothy (1867–1942) married Nancy Laderoute; St. Pierre (1870–1918) married Rosalie Campion; Madeline (1872–1946) married Norbert L'Hirondelle; Caroline Clara (1874–1920) married George Rodgers; Sévère (1876–1904) married Louise Belcourt; Benjamin (1878–?) married Rosalie Campion, Marianne Courtepatte, and Emilie Desjarlais; Adelaide (1882–?)

Alexis Belcourt (1826–1881) and Nancy Rowand (1836–) had the following children: Sophie (1849–1934) married Louis Courtereille; Alexander (1852–1915) married Madeline Gladu; Christianne (1855–1953) married Baptiste Letendre; Louisa (1858–?) married John Horatio Nelson Brazeau; Victoria Anne (1861–1966) married Louis Jerome Callihoo; Athanese (1865–1870); Virginie (1867–?) married Isaac Gagnon then J. Fisher; Joseph (1871–1888); John (1875–?) married Maggie Fraser; Mary Jane Euphrasine (1882–?); Elizabeth Finlay (adopted) (1877–?) married Tom Auger and Solomon Berland.

Louis and Victoria experienced many changes in their lifestyle. As the years went by, wood stoves replaced mud fireplaces in the home, and the white mud wash on the interior was replaced by wallpaper. People had better furniture, cooking pots and dishes. There was enamelware for cooking and it was commonly used for everyday dishes. You could save up for luxurious things, such as a crucifix for the wall or a wind-up phonograph. The phonograph inspired ingenuity. A natural thorn from a plant worked as a needle for playing records. More kinds of vegetables began to be planted. For example, in 1892 on the Enoch Reserve, gardens contained celery, red cabbage, pumpkins, tomatoes, corn, and tobacco in addition to the more ordinary potatoes, turnips, beans and peas. They also grew hemp, flax, buckwheat, wheat, oats and barley.[26] Flour could be milled at Fort Edmonton, and later at St. Albert, so people could make bannock and bake bread. Even so, houses remained small, there were numerous children and most people were obliged to find other paid work to supplement the poor living made from the farm. Poverty was a common plight of Métis people. Many families moved around from one place to the other in the hope of finding a living, either by obtaining enough good land or the opportunity to work. Perhaps they were optimistic. It couldn't get worse—maybe another place would offer a better chance. Making a living by hunting bison was no longer an option.

In an effort to save the plains bison from extinction. Father Lacombe wrote to a federal employee, Morris, in 1875, with advice about the Indians.[22i] He said that the government should prohibit hunting of bison in the winter and the selling of the meat for food for five years. People would then be forced to provide for themselves in other ways and, indeed, could do so if the government gave them guns with ammunition and lent them nets for fishing. He also thought it would encourage the Indians to engage in agriculture if they were supplied with livestock and implements. Already in the 1870s bison had become harder to get. The *Saskatchewan Herald* had a report from Edmonton in 1878 that Narcisse Beaudry went hunting bison on the plains for a month and returned empty-handed. The *Edmonton Bulletin* mentioned that one of the last successful plains bison hunts took place in January 1882.

By the time the bison were too scarce to be a reliable food source, there was also a great increase in the population out West due to new homesteaders. Incoming pioneers who were already experienced farmers were often able to compete successfully with the local people. But it was absolutely necessary to take up farming. It was such a struggle. First, people had to cut down the trees, dig up the roots and stones and dig the soil by hand. To farm effectively you had to have the inclination, some luck with the climate, appropriate seed, and some costly machinery. Equipment and seed were hard to come by. The Mission at St. Albert gave out seed in 1889 to certain reliable inhabitants such as Samuel Cunningham, Edwin Belcourt, the Savard brothers and Jean Baptiste Belcourt on condition that they return twice the amount at harvest.[68 xii]

One of the earliest and nearly the sole employer was the Hudson's Bay Company. Trapping was an important source of income for people, on a small scale, or even as a way of making a living. The Hudson's Bay Company built a store at St. Albert in 1866. No wonder we don't see many lynx in the region today, for in one year alone, 1867, they obtained 500 pelts! The St. Albert Mission also sold goods and food in competition with merchants. Its account books for the 1870s show that many people bartered labour at the Mission for the things they needed. For example, two of Michel Callihoo's nephews, Felix Savard, and Leon Delorme, and a brother-in-law, Alexander Savard were employed here.[67 viii] The work available from the Mission in St. Albert included construction, farm labour, freighting to Red River and accompanying priests on trips. By the 1880s, people switched to paying for goods with cash, grain or wood.[68 xi] Some even brought wool to sell, which indicates that by this time sheep were being raised.

Louis Jerome's cousins Louis and Michel Callihoo did not prosper right after they took scrip. They were described by Corporal Bossauge of the Northwest Mounted Police, in early January of 1889, as being "very hard up and having nothing for the winter." By this time, both men had families to support. Their elder brother, Joseph, was more fortunate as he was working for the police at Fort Saskatchewan. The Government through the Police, regularly provided relief rations during the winter to needy "half-breeds". For instance, on March 1 of that same year, they doled out 871 pounds of flour and 261 pounds of bacon to 173 people, many of whom were also Michel's relatives.

As time went on various industries required men to labour as freighters. Guides were still needed in the hinterland. As companies began to explore and prospect for minerals, many jobs entailed being away from home for long periods. It must have been very hard on family life.

In order to make some extra money, Victoria reportedly worked as a cook on a survey outfit just north of St. Albert. Here she learned to make loaf bread and memorable baked beans. On the Reserve Louis had a mixed farm where they had horses, and raised cattle, hogs, chickens and turkeys. They also kept sheep until coyotes killed too many of them. Victoria used to spin the wool to knit socks and mitts.

Louis built a good new house in 1890.[29] The Callihoos owned a steam threshing outfit with a hand feed and a straw carrier separator. They had to hire men to run the machinery until their son Vital Victor graduated from industrial school with the skills to do the job. The enterprising couple also bought a sawmill.

Louis and Victoria did not get a chance to learn to read and write but were keen on schooling for their children. They sent the children to the St. Joseph's Industrial School (known as Dunbow) near High River. Anne and Dio went first, probably in November of 1885, but after visiting them the following August, their parents took them home. Dio was back at school by February 1889, and was mentioned in the school journal because he got into trouble. He stayed until he was nineteen and graduated in blacksmithing and farming. He was described as "intelligent and a good worker". It was William's turn to come to school in 1889 along with his cousin Johnny while two older Callihoo boys went home having learned farming. William graduated at eighteen with a Level Four in farming. His first wife, Anne English, a girl from the Peigan Nation, was discharged at the same time. Adolphus and John didn't do as well as Victor and Henry who achieved a Level Five on leaving. However, the assistant principal expressed a high opinion of all the Callihoos. They represented about a third of the small student body in the 1880s[68]!

Louis and Victoria lost two baby girls in infancy. They also lost their seventeen-year-old son, John, just after he left school. In a shocking industrial accident at the family saw mill, his pocket became entangled and he was pulled into the blade. His parents were impelled to get rid of the mill and move from the site of the tragedy.

At this point in their lives, Louis and Victoria sold their stock and equipment and built a new house at Lac Ste-Anne. Here they raised cattle and sold dairy products. They then bought and operated what was known as a temperance hotel with a coffee shop. Even school teachers felt safe staying there.

Louis and Victoria moved back to the Reserve in 1921. By this time most of their children were grown up and married. William had joined the army for W.W. I and come back. When Louis Jerome died of cancer in 1926, Victoria stayed for a while, and then made her home at Lac Ste-Anne. She later lived near her daughter Hermine Vandalle at Gunn for a time until she finally moved to the Youville Home in St. Albert. Victoria was able to see about 150 great-grandchildren grow up and is remembered by everyone who met her as a very vigorous and intelligent person. She was well known for her ability as a Native healer but she also believed in the curative powers of the waters of Lac Ste-Anne. She was famous for her talent and pleasure at dancing, even at an advanced age! Her family and friends honoured her on her hundredth birthday with a fine party. After dinner she had a rest, and later she stepped onto the dance floor! It wasn't until she was 104 that she died and was buried beside her husband in the Villeneuve cemetery.

All but two of Louis' brothers were farmers on the Michel Reserve. Many other members of the family, such as cousin Joseph and two of his brothers, obtained "half-breed" scrip in 1885, and in 1894 Thomas' sons

---

Louis Jerome and Victoria had the following children: Anne (1879–1969) married Stoney Boris then Jean Baptiste Loyer; D'o Leon (1880–1944); Hermine "Lizzie" (1881–?) married Ben Vandalle; William (1883–1954) married Anne English then Anne Gairdner; Adolphus (1885–1967) married Christine Breland then Louise Bellerose and Eliza; Vital Victor (1888–972) married Clothilde Hodgson; Henry (1879–1939) married Clara Loyer; Alice (1895–1975) married Charles Baird; Caroline (1897–1897); Melvina (1897–1898); John (1898–1915); Julia Mary (1901–?) married Wilfred Laderoute; Bertha Victoire (1903–?) married F. Kildaw, then Larry Dennis, then Roderick Letendre.

Plate 18. Victoria Callihoo's 100th birthday. From left, her children: Lizzie Vandelle, Adolphus Callihoo, Annie Boris, May Laderoute, Alice Baird around Victoria, seated.
courtesy Lac Ste-Anne Historical Society

William and Elzéar obtained theirs. Isabelle and Josephine were denied as was St. Pierre.[22 xxi] For some, if you couldn't make a living on the Reserve, you could get scrip and sell it for some ready cash. But there was no going back.

Some of Louis Jerome's cousins were also farmers near St. Albert or elsewhere in the district. For example, his first cousin, Michel, farmed near Rivière-Qui-Barre. The North attracted people too. A popular area that opened up in the early part of the 1900s for work and for farming as well was the Peace River region and this is where another first cousin, also called Louis, went by pack horse in 1896 after leaving the Reserve and endeavouring to make a living at St. Albert and then Lesser Slave Lake. This Louis finally became quite famous as an early pioneer of Grande Prairie. Here, he and his son Henry cut and hauled logs for the First Protestant Church which is now at the Grande Prairie Pioneer Museum. Louis spoke English, French, Cree and Beaver, and was an interpreter for a time for the North West Mounted Police. He and his sons also worked on freight wagons.[80]

Cousin Adam, along with his brother, William, and three of their sisters' families, the Gladus and Letendres and other close relations, some Grays and Belcourts, chose to go north too. At Kelly Lake, B.C., these families formed the backbone of a growing community.[3]. Here there was a frontier lifestyle and people were employed for their knowledge of the country and their ability to speak Cree and other Native languages. In the north and out west near the mountains as well, the Karakonti descendants of Louis Callihoo raised horses and used them to make a living as guides and outfitters. They also sustained themselves with hunting in addition to minimal farms. Most rural families made some extra money trapping fur animals. Outside opportunities presented themselves in the form of mining and exploration. With settlement came jobs on the railways, building highways and construction in the towns. By the end of the nineteenth century there were a few major fur merchants and trappers

---

Aileen Perrault says she loved being with Victoria and visited her often, even though the old lady spoke almost no English and Aileen spoke no Cree. She also says that Victoria had trained her cat to catch grouse and bring them home and that the dog would bring in firewood on request.

competing with the Hudson's Bay Company. One of these was the first Louis Callihoo's grandson, Pierre Gray, who operated out of Jasper and later at Lac Ste-Anne and Island Lake.

The Métis who made their homes in what is now Jasper National Park had filed no homestead claims. They were considered to be squatters by the Government and were required to move around 1910 when the park was established. Some of their descendants now live in the area of Grande Cache or Hinton.

School Days

Louis Jerome's younger brothers and sisters also went to the industrial school at Dunbow. Even Timothy was here although he was no longer a child in 1885. He was kept busy drawing water and breaking out ice to be stored for the summer in –44°F. weather in January. He also cut wood and sheared sheep. He had to work on the farm most of the time, it seems. He is described in the journal as "giddy and lazy" but very intelligent. St. Pierre, although nineteen, went along with his family one year because he wanted to learn the trade of carpenter and was accepted at the school. After barely twenty-four hours he rushed away to rejoin the rest of the family who had gone to Calgary. Eleven-year-old Sévère was there in 1886, and in January, 1889 he was chosen to read the New Year's address. He learned enough to teach school at the Alexis Reserve. Caroline attended the school for a few years and Benjamin also took his turn. Louis' nephew, Solomon Timothy, and possibly his brothers also attended Dunbow along with their cousins.[68 vi]

At school they had lessons most mornings and worked in the afternoon at tasks around the institution and at various trades. Steam engineering became important after the turn of the century and was taught at the school by a professional. Students all had to work hard, chopping wood, improving roads, digging potatoes, chopping ice, and helping in the bakery. In the fall the older boys took in 2,500 tons of hay. They also did their own laundry and cleaning. At school, the students used English most of the time and perhaps learned to speak a little Blackfoot. Although they attended school with siblings and cousins, the separation from home was very hard on them and on their parents, too, as the school was so far away. Henry said he was home only twice in ten years! Sometimes in the summer Louis and Victoria would travel down with a wagon and team of horses to visit their children. The trip took a week. They would then camp on the school grounds. This was also a good opportunity to visit Victoria's sister, Mrs. Louisa Brazeau, in Calgary. After 1902, visits by Callihoo parents are no longer mentioned in the school journals.[68 vi] The students were able to travel back and forth by stage coach between Calgary and Edmonton and after 1891, they could make an exciting trip by train!

School must have been fun as well as hard work. There were dancing lessons and singing classes and the boys could perform with the band. In 1893, the band played in the Calgary Parade and at the Opera House! Sometimes the students would watch a Magic Lantern show. During an Epiphany pageant, in 1900, seven-year-old Willie was crowned one of the kings. Henry travelled to different Alberta towns with the hockey team that year. The kids got to visit Calgary and see the Exhibition. One year the boys were taken to the Circus. The boys could play fastball, shoot gophers, fish for trout and swim in the river in their spare time. They could even try to walk on stilts. Summer camp-outs were arranged and everyone was taken on picnics. On the occasion of the visit to Calgary by the Duke and Duchess of Cornwall, sixty students from Dunbow were taken to the ceremony at Shaganappi Point in the fall of 1901.[67 v] Louis' boys were in this group, according to Vital Callihoo. Here they saw a thousand Native people, many of whom were colourfully dressed with their faces painted, and wearing feathered headdresses.[27]

Many of the young people born after 1870 were sent to the Grey Nuns Convent in St. Albert. This was a boarding school which concentrated on manual labour for Native students. Some of the families on the Michel Reserve registered the children of non-Treaty relatives as their own to give these kids a chance to go to school free.

The Grey Nuns built a convent at St. Albert and began teaching school there in 1863. Here, girls were taught household arts and were kept busy with the cleaning and laundry of the institution. One young orphan, Betsy Callihoo, was in and out of the convent her whole young life and was never taught to read and write. She became a wise and competent adult in spite of it. The boys had to work in the fields and tend the livestock.

Indian students had their fees paid by the government which made regular inspections. In August 1884, an Inspector from the Department of Indian Affairs reported that the older children were doing the harvest. No wonder he found the place neat and clean as the girls spent much of their time doing housework. Most of the students must have at least learned their 'three Rs', because he also says that they passed a "very creditable examination." The girls had carded and spun wool and made flannel by dyeing and weaving and there was also knitting and fancy work.[23 vi] Inspector Wadsworth visited the school in 1887, and said that the children had improved in their studies, but again that the older children were engaged in "industrial pursuits connected with the institution." He remarked that any day the Sisters would move into their new residence which Father Leduc said cost nearly forty thousand dollars. This time the inspector found a great discrepancy in the accounts for supplies and food.[23 xii] One has the impression that the students may not have received what the government had paid for on their behalf.

People have told stories of the cruelty or unfairness of some of the Sisters. What was even more degrading than that was the fundamental institutional attitude. The children deemed to be 'native' were strictly segregated from those who were 'white'. They were not allowed to eat together, worship together nor to sleep in the same dormitories. They were even beaten for sneaking out and playing with one another. The students met only in the classroom where slower students were humiliated. The racism displayed was more extreme than that displayed by the general public. For instance, all of the St. Albert school trustees elected in the fall of 1886 were Métis. Pascal Breland and Samuel Cunningham, both Métis, were appointed to represent St. Albert at the Northwest Territories Council in the 1880s, while Edmonton citizens elected William Rowland, who was Métis, as a trustee, to its very first school board.

The first public school in St. Albert opened in 1884. Soon afterwards, small schools were built to accommodate the children whose homes were scattered throughout the general region. In 1885, the plans included St. Leon School on the St. Albert Road, another in town near the Mission, the Bellerose School to the east and the Cunningham School in the west. Many students could only go to school if they could get there on foot, and they were allowed to stay in school only until they were needed to help at home. Most people spoke a local version of Cree at home. Many also spoke French quite regularly.

St. Albert

The Métis citizens of St. Albert formulated a fine set of laws and chose constables and a magistrate as early as 1863. Other major developments in the community included a bridge across the Sturgeon River, a saw mill, a grist mill, general stores and hotels. At one time, there was even a pemmican factory.

The settlement suffered from epidemics in the 1870s and near starvation in the 1880s. In the winter of 1888, federal police authorities had to provide relief for more than 140 people. Contributing to the difficulties experienced by the Métis were governmental restrictions on hunting and trapping. The people of Lac Ste-Anne were obliged to purchase fishing licences from the 1890s on, which they considered a hardship. In June 1893, they had a meeting at which they decided to petition the government to revoke the licence law as they hadn't the means to pay and had no other support but fish.

Ownership and title to land in St. Albert nearly became a problem. The Hudson's Bay Company, which had control before Confederation, had not been too concerned about land occupancy. A new Canadian government

---

Mabel went to the convent at the age of eight. She said that even dogs wouldn't eat the food. Although one Sister was "wonderful", she said they made you work all the time. You had to scrub floors and darn socks and if the darning wasn't done right, they made you unpick the socks and do them again. She said she "doesn't have a good word for the nuns." She said the people treated worst were the orphans. She also added that her parents never came to visit, and that, anyway, there was no love at home, either. She was taken out of school every time they needed her at home to look after the other children and to do housework, especially when her mother had a new baby. She said that her father was also "mean".

Hector was sent to the convent at the age of five. He said he had to milk cows and clean barns and, thus, didn't learn much. He said there wasn't enough food, never any milk or butter, although these things were produced on the farm. When the inspector came from the government, milk and butter appeared on the table set for the occasion on unaccustomed white tablecloths, but if you took any, you got a beating.

had a plan for surveying the land that was at odds with the river lot system established by the Métis settlers, not only here but at Lac Ste-Anne and Edmonton. The government favoured the grid system which arranged square mile sections in orderly townships. However, because of pressure put on the government by local politicians and Father Lacombe, the survey was done, and patents awarded according to local custom. The unsettled remainder was then surveyed in the grid system. The government also passed the Homestead Act in 1872 that had strict requirements. You had to clear ten acres and build a home within three years before you could acquire title of ownership to a quarter section (160 acres).

Daily Life

Most of those young women who married farmers of the region had similar lives to those of their mothers. Michel's daughter, Corinne, made a more romantic marriage by becoming the wife of the Count de Pierpont and emigrating to his chateau in France. In the *Edmonton Bulletin* of October 27, 1898, is a description of a splendid Métis wedding at Lesser Slave Lake when Louis Callihoo's daughter, Philomène, married St. Pierre Ferguson. The bride wore a white dress and rode in a decorated carriage while a whole procession of colourful carriages was accompanied by deafening gunfire salutes which continued until there was no ammunition left. The whole community attended and the guests managed to consume three steers and twenty bushels of potatoes amongst many other good things. They danced and ate for 36 hours straight and the fiddlers wore out fifteen violin strings!

During the twentieth century, most Métis people in the central part of Alberta had a rural lifestyle that is familiar to most of those who have read local histories or have listened to grandparents' stories. People lived on farms in order to provide the basic necessities of life for their large families, even if they had businesses or other employment. Such small farms demanded an endless round of heavy daily chores for each member of the family. Some produce, especially cream and home-made butter, was sold in order to obtain cash. Even in town people kept some livestock or chickens and planted large vegetable gardens. Men and boys took all kinds of jobs to earn some money. Ernie Callihoo remembers pulling stumps when he was only eight years old to help his family. In most ways, their lives were like those of non-Natives living under similar circumstances. Some farms were successful businesses. If you could hire a large threshing crew, and had the machinery, as Solomon Callihoo did, you went around from farm to farm at harvest time which was quite profitable.

Solomon and Elizabeth Callihoo

Solomon, sometimes called Solomon Dick after his maternal grandfather, Chief Michel's oldest son in his second family, was born at Lac Ste-Anne in 1874 and was raised on the Michel Reserve #132. He went to boarding school at Dunbow from 1885 until 1890. Here he distinguished himself, especially in mathematics, and was usually the top student. In addition, Solomon got to work in the school bakery when he was twelve. He also learned carpentry. Solomon enjoyed the church services in Latin and not only was an altar boy at school, but served Mass later on in the church at St. Albert.

He is described in the school journals as being proud and as one who did not believe that he ought to be punished when he did something naughty at school. The assistant principal gave his high rank to another boy to encourage Solomon to apply himself better in order to regain his position. His reward, in the autumn, was a visit to Calgary. Solomon later became temperamental again and had to be punished; however, he was still a good student and conducted the school when the assistant principal was sick in February 1889. He wrote English very well, too, and a journal describes his writing as bringing no discredit to a person who had been there twice as long. The writing referred to in particular was a letter to his father asking to be taken home.[67 v] Solomon went home for good that summer. He later told his daughter that it was because his father missed him although the school had been told he had to help out on the farm.

As a young man Solomon was employed on the Sotaert farm near Villeneuve. Although he stood out at school he grew up to be a quiet person. In 1902, Solomon married Elizabeth Plante who was a very forceful and intelligent lady. Her mother was descended from Francis Xavier

Plante and from Belcourts and L'Hirondelles. Elizabeth had been brought up in the household of her stepfather, John Norris, in Edmonton. She could speak French and English and could play the piano. She also spoke Cree and was very capable in essential Native life skills needed on the Reserve. She had the reputation of being an excellent midwife and nurse and was frequently called in to help sick people. She also had the reputation of being able to "bring the roof down" at church when she sang!

One of the major scourges of the first half of the twentieth century was tuberculosis. Of their twelve children, Elizabeth and Solomon lost seven, some as infants, and others as teens or young adults—mostly from this disease. Their daughter, Beatrice, also contracted it but recovered at the Sanitarium in Edmonton.

On the farm they had a dairy operation and raised Yorkshire hogs. They also had two teams of four horses for freighting and harvest. When starting out as a farmer, Solomon needed machinery. He went to the Massey Harris company to get a binder (called a "reaper") on credit. They decided to trust him and were not disappointed. Solomon had such a good reputation that he was able to get machinery when others may have found it difficult. It is said that there was a note in his file at Massey-Harris saying, "name as good as gold." He was a good businessman and listened faithfully to the daily agricultural market reports on the radio. When he couldn't tune in, one of his children had to do so and was obliged to keep good notes.

Solomon was Headman on the Michel Reserve in his cousin Louis' day and became Chief of the Michel Band from 1917 to 1935. He finally retired to a small house at the nearby town of Calahoo and died in Edmonton in 1967.

Fred and Mary Callihoo

Fred Callihoo was one of the more successful farmers on the Michel Reserve. Born in 1900, he was a son of Timothy Callihoo and Nancy Laderoute whose grandfather, Olivier Seguin *dit* Laderoute was from Montreal and whose other ancestors were Dumonts and L'Hirondelles. Fred went to school down at Dunbow, and afterwards may have worked

Plate 19. Solomon and Elizabeth Callihoo, ca. 1940
courtesy Beatrice Callihoo

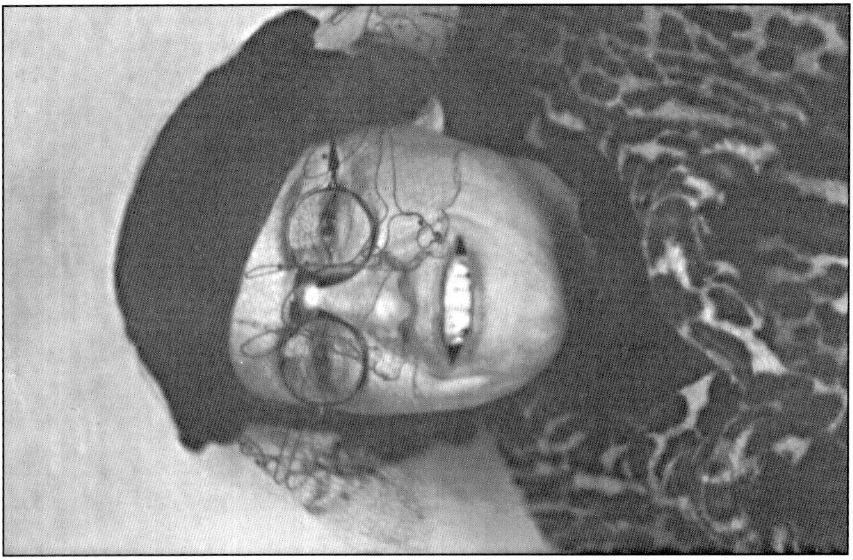

Plate 20. Freddie Callihoo ca. 1930 *courtesy Musée Héritage Museum*
Plate 21. Mary Valerie Callihoo ca. 1900 *courtesy Musée Héritage Museum*

on his dad's farm until he married. Mary Valerie, the widow of a Louis Dumont, who died of Spanish flu in 1918. She was from St. Albert, a daughter of James Cunningham and Mary Hodgson, and descended from L'Hirondelles and Rowlands. She was very lively and bright even at 99 years of age, and described how, at the age of thirteen, she persuaded her father to send her to the convent because there was no school within walking distance. Even though she spent most of her year there working at menial tasks, she learned her 'three Rs'.

Fred and Mary married in 1931. They both worked hard in their fields and kept a flock of 500 chickens. Mary Callihoo, even in her old age, clearly remembered the role of the farm wife who prepared one gargantuan meal after another for all the men at harvest time! They also raised hogs. Fred and Mary were able to afford a two story frame house at a time when most people on the Reserve still built theirs of logs. People recall her wonderful flower garden to this day. She also planted apple and plum trees which were bought as four-foot saplings from a travelling salesman. They adopted a son, Joe, who later married Mildred Arcand. Fred is remembered for a nasty accident. He once walked into the propeller of a small plane after having had a few drinks. He had enjoyed his $2-for-fifteen-minutes ride and jumped out of the plane and ran around the front to line up for another turn. He was just lucky the propeller was barely moving. Even so, it is said that he needed 151 stitches.

Fred became Chief of the Michel Reserve from 1936 to 1948. He died in 1958 and is buried at Villeneuve. Mary moved to the town of Calahoo. She lived past her one hundredth birthday, ending her days in a small old-folks' home at the Alexander Reserve in 1994.

Solomon and Elizabeth Plante (1884–1955) had the following children: Jimmy (1903–1906); Dicky (1905–1905); Catherine Elizabeth (1907–1907); Thomas (1909–1984) married Rose Lucille Berry; Arthur (1910–1992); Edith (1912–1936); John (1916–1916); Malcolm Fred (1917–1934); Jeannette (1919–1938); Emily (1921–) married Dan Mitchell; Beatrice Gladys (1922–) married Alex Montrose Callihoo; Lloyd (1924–994) married Kathleen Callihoo.

Finding Work

A few people with special skills or education went into business. An example was a grandnephew of Michel Callihoo, Ambroise Gray, who opened a barber shop and pool hall in the town of Lac Ste-Anne. Louis Jerome's son-in-law, Stoney Boris, had a similar business. Many men had to earn wages wherever they found an opportunity. They might work as carpenters for a time or on construction. They sometimes had to walk for miles to get to a work site. They hired out to pull stumps or clear brush: sometimes they were lucky enough to get a more interesting job on a survey crew. Jean Felix was engaged to guide a party of more than twenty people whom the *Bulletin* describes as "Californians" as far as Fort St. John, on their way to the Gold Rush in the Yukon, in August 1897. Johnny and Adolphus also had exciting jobs guiding people to the Klondike Gold Rush. Johnny later became a postman. There were those who were bitten by the 'gold bug' and could make some money panning for gold. Two Callihoos panned gold in October 1895 on the shore of the North Saskatchewan near Edmonton for good 'pay' (which is what you could make a day by selling the flakes of gold you found).[26] Some people moved freight with horses—others used boats. Charles Beauregard, a Callihoo descendent, was a freighter out of St. Paul des Métis who floated goods by scow or flat boat down the North Saskatchewan from Edmonton. Making a living was only one consideration, as men started to be concerned about settling down where their children could be educated properly. If you had no land, or couldn't make a living by farming you were hard put to find

---

Timothy Callihoo (1868–1942) and Nancy Laderoute (1874–1949) had the following children: Wilfred (1893–1893); Jean Baptiste (1894–894); Solomon Timothy (1898–?) married Charlotte Fife; Agnes (?–?); Alfred John (1900–1958) married Mary Valerie Cunningham; Victor McClure (1906–?) married Beatrice L'Hirondelle; Mary Anne (1912–?); Delia Delina (1914–?);

James Cunningham (1854–1940) and Mary Hodgson (1859–1930) had the following children: Elizabeth (1880–1976) married Joseph Dion; Sophie (1881–1960) married Johnny Callihoo; William George (1884–?) married Virginie Trottier; Hermine (1886–?) married Innes Gairdner; Napoleon John (1888–1910); Frederick (?–?); Mary Valerie (1893–1994) married Louis Dumont then Fred Callihoo; Margaret Alice (1894–?); Rachel (1895–?) married George Loyer then William Callihoo; Robert (1898–?); Clara Mary Louise (1900–?) married Henry Loyer.

some kind of job. Napoleon Calliou worked on equipment for a southern ranch, while Ernie and Hector Callihoo and Gilbert Anderson, first cousins, mined coal. Men found jobs as teamsters, in steel mills and fighting forest fires. Henry Callihoo made railway ties for seven cents apiece. Those with a better education had more choice. Patrick became an Indian Agent and his sister Dolly a school teacher.

Most women, if they went out to work at all, became domestics in hotels and other such institutions. They worked as waitresses and had cleaning jobs. Elizabeth Cunningham, an in-law of the Callihoos, was a trained practical nurse. Josephine Callihoo Laderoute taught school at Hobbema Reserve before she got married in 1893,[25] and at Fish Creek in about 1906 when her children were still young. Many housewives supplemented the family's income by making butter and other dairy products and taking them around to sell. Some women were prepared to put in the hours of work required to make moccasins for between 25 cents and 50 cents a pair. Even in the store, in 1894, they sold for only 50 cents to $2.50.[27]

Before the turn of the century, young men of this generation could still have an exciting life with adventures not unlike those of their voyageur ancestors. Some actively supported the Métis cause in 1885. There were others, such as the citizens of St. Albert, who were very concerned with the safety of their community and joined the St. Albert Mounted Rifles.

St. Albert Mounted Rifles

Citizens rallied together in 1885 when they formed the St. Albert Mounted Rifles. This was one of the local militias formed to defend the region from attack should the Riel Rebellion against the government spill over into Alberta from Saskatchewan.

It is not known if Michel Callihoo was involved with the Rebellion of 1885. He must have been very concerned if only because so many of his relatives were in the volunteer army formed to protect St. Albert citizens against potential attack. The Captain, Samuel Cunningham, was the husband of Michel Callihoo's niece, Suzanne, and the Sergeant, Magloire Gray, was her brother. Michel's son Michel, four other nephews, a son-in-law, François Boudreau, his granddaughter's husband, Noel

Delorme, and a half dozen other relatives and connections were also amongst the soldiers.

According to Father Lestanc of the Alexander Reserve, trouble in the regions close to Edmonton was started by a letter reportedly written by Louis Riel, the famous Métis revolutionary, to the chiefs of various reserves inciting them to revolt against the government. He told them not to harm the Métis and not to listen to their priests who had "always blindfolded them." One local disturbance was on April 14 when the people of the Alexis Reserve attacked the store at nearby Lac Ste-Anne and on the nineteenth did war dances, demanded food and goods and carried on all night. When the chief showed up he said he had received a letter as described from Louis Riel but didn't want to make war. Even though he did not reprove his rowdy young men, it didn't go any further and Bishop Grandin sent Chief Alexis a message congratulating him on having listened to his priest.[68 iv]

On April 17, 1885, came the news of a battle at Frog Lake. It was followed by some violence further south by the Cree on a reserve on the North Saskatchewan. Disagreeable events multiplied over the months of April and May and many citizens of Fort Saskatchewan and Edmonton became so frightened that a few of them took refuge in St. Albert.[68 iv]

The Métis in St. Albert and area must have been in sympathy with the cause of the Métis of the East and their leader, Louis Riel, and Gabriel Dumont, his lieutenant. However their concern was for the safety and indeed the reputation of their own community. Some prominent Métis citizens wrote a letter to the newspaper to this effect.[27]

> To the Editor of the BULLETIN
>
> Sir. - The following statement appears in the Winnipeg Weekly Sun newspaper of the 25th ult.:
>
> "The Hudson's Bay Company received a telegram from their agent at Edmonton last night stating that the half-breeds there were holding secret meetings for some time, and are now organizing for action of some kind. Trouble is expected at once."
>
> We cannot adequately express the indignation we feel at the reading of such a despatch. Undoubtedly we have many reasons for complaining against the government, and those who accuse us cannot say we are wrong. They know best the rights that we have to the lands of the country. We are aborigines as well as Indians and have the same rights as they. Before any of those foreigners, whom the government to-day prefers to us, saw the country we had begun to cultivate

it. The company who are reported to have sold our country would willingly have sold us as well. Had they more rights than we? The government understood that the Indians had rights in this country and consequently made treaties with them but with us half-breeds what treaties have been made? What favour have they conferred on us? Let a single case be instanced. Far from receiving favors, we have not been accorded fair play. Last summer a government agent came here to settle a local land question and had it been his aim to provoke the halfbreeds to rebellion he could not have devised better means than his decisions, which were always so manifestly unjust to them. Give an instance between a half-breed and a foreigner where the half-breed was not sacrificed. In many cases half-breeds who were long settled in their homes of their own have seen their lands taken from them and portioned out to newly arrived strangers and those men are thus forced to make way for foreigners, locating again to be very probably dispossessed later in the same way. Do they believe we have no feelings? We feel those wrongs deeply. Our complaints heretofore have not found expression beyond ourselves. We ask you today to publish them in your column for the first time. We have never thought of rebellion or inciting to rebellion. How under such circumstances have these strangers the arrogance to ask us to take up arms in defense of them and theirs? Were we indeed what they think us we would take arms in truth , but for the purpose of enforcing justice to ourselves. We would be expected by them to take sides with the half-breeds at Duck Lake whose rising we condemn and deplore we would be expected to join the discontented Indians. Men who know the influence of the half-breeds over the Indians will readily accept the continued good behaviour of the Indians round about us as the strongest evidence of our loyalty. We wish to state that instead of siding with blood-thirsty Indians we are ready to take arms against those monsters who dare spill the blood of defenseless people, not sparing even the lives of our priests. As a rule no Half-Breed ever treats a stranger with injustice, contempt or even incivility the treatment a Half-Breed gives to a stranger, has he not a right to demand from the stranger? There are in this district many strangers who have deservedly our good will and who are as indignant as we are at the injustice of the malignant accusation we are complaining of. In conclusion we ask all newspapers who are friends of justice to publish this our protest against the above slander dispatched to Winnipeg by the agent of the Hudson's Bay Company at Edmonton.

(Signed) Samuel Cunningham, Octave Bellerose, John Cunningham, Baptiste Courtepatte, John Rowland, Adolphus Rowland, Louis Chastellaine, Lawrence Gurness, on behalf of the Half-Breeds of St. Albert, Saint Albert, Alberta, April 21st, 1885.

The St. Albert Mounted Rifles was formed on May 16. Eighty-five percent of the forty fellows who enlisted were Métis. Their Captain was Samuel Cunningham with Dan Maloney as his Sergeant. Ironically, the first cousin of the famous revolutionary Gabriel Dumont, called Felix Dumont, signed up as a Private in this troop. The government armed them with Snider Enfield rifles. Under the command of Lieutenant Des Georges of Number 2 Company 65th Regiment they made one trip northeastward on June 9, 1885.[27] This was in order to come to the aid of the people of Lac la Biche because it was rumoured that Big Bear, an Indian leader, and two thousand men were going to attack. Fortunately there was no bloodshed and they all came safely home.

Callihoos and The Law

The Callihoos and their relatives seemed to be law-abiding, for the most part. They certainly had a good reputation with the Indian Agents over the years, as being unusually moral. A few Métis came before the magistrate Mr. Gairdner in St. Albert for horse stealing or drunkenness but most stayed out of trouble. The Callihoos did have a few brushes with the law, however. The *Edmonton Bulletin* of April 15, 1882, reported on a court hearing in which Jean Felix is accused of shooting W.J. O'Donnell's cow. (Mr. O'Donnell was the farm instructor paid by the Department of Indian Affairs on the Alexander Reserve.) Jean Felix admitted to shooting the cow. His father, Jean Baptiste, and uncle, Michel, said they heard him threatening to shoot the first government animal he saw because the agent had refused him Relief. Jean Felix brought the meat to Michel's house to have it cooked. They refused to cook it there but shared in the meal after Jean Felix had it cooked at his own place. The police found the head, hide and some meat at the culprit's house. The reporter described Jean Felix, saying that his deportment and dress were like that of a white man and that he could speak English, French and Cree. The paper later reported an attempted rape by someone called Cunningham on the Michel Reserve.

We most often hear of men's adventures with dangerous wild animals. Here is a story about some brave women taken from the *Bulletin* of December 1, 1898: An eighty-year-old lady, Mrs. Harnois, from Lac Ste-Anne, knew where there was a bear in its den. She and two other women including Eliza Omowaskew, Jean Felix Calihoo's wife, took a rope and a gun and went to kill it. The bear was part way out of its den when Eliza quickly grabbed its hind paw and fastened one end of the rope to it before it could get away. She tied the other end to a tree. Mrs. Harnois then shot the bear.

Plate 22. *front right:* Magloire Belcourt, son of Cecile Callihoo, and wife Christine, probably her father, Jean Baptiste "Mooswa" Letendre with unidentified young people
photo Ernest Brown, Provincial Archives of Alberta

Plate 23. *from left:* Norbert and Jeanne Callioux, daughter, Jessie, Big Pat Callihoo, his parents, Sophie and Johnny Callihoo, Wedding, 1935 *courtesy St. Albert Historical Society*

There was an incident at St. Albert in 1896 in which people from the Michel Reserve joined with their friends and relatives to commit an act for which they were arrested by the police. Fifty-six men were charged for having "unlawfully, routously, riotously, tumultuously assembled together to the disturbance of the public peace, and did unlawfully, and with force, demolish and pull down certain buildings, to wit a dwelling house and stable." This mob wanted to get rid of a man whom they believed to be a squatter on disputed hay lands near Big Lake, and to send a strong message to other potential squatters.[27] Of the men involved in this incident, there were twelve people from the Reserve and dozens of their St. Albert relations. Four of Michel's sons, his brother Jean Baptiste, some nephews, a son-in-law, and his brother-in-law 'Muchas' Collin, were among the participants. The outcome wasn't reported but it is noteworthy how the members of the Métis community organized to act together in this way.

Spanish Influenza

While some diseases were being controlled, there were occasional epidemics of new ones. The Spanish influenza, reportedly spread by W.W. I soldiers in 1918, afflicted the whole western world. There was no cure and some whole families succumbed to it. In St. Albert they made it compulsory to wear face masks for a time to try to prevent its spread. Jean Felix, most of his family, and his cousin Albert were only a few of its victims.

Political Action

In this generation were also bred some politicians and statesmen who devoted themselves to the rights of Native people. Johnny Callihoo was the first president of the Indian Association of Alberta. His younger brother, Felix, devoted himself to alleviating the economic plight of Métis people. He served on the first board of the Métis Association of Alberta when Joseph Dion was President. A quote follows from a speech Felix delivered on December 28, 1932, "Our first objective and the one in which we have our deepest interest, the one which more than anything else called our movement into being, is to see that adequate provision is made for our homeless and destitute families ... to see that proper provision is made for the education of our children [and] also provision of a better system of medical attention." Felix had originally studied for the priesthood along with his friend Edward Cunningham but changed his mind and actually turned against the clergy and its influence.

Settlements

At the turn of the century, Métis people still had very large families and it was hard to make ends meet. The flood of settlers from Europe, eastern Canada and the United States made for competition and population pressure. The government began to impose restrictions on hunting and fishing. Poverty was even worse during the Great Depression of the 1930s. Ernie Callihoo remembers that a side of beef was once 'accidentally' dropped off the train by someone who knew of the destitution. He said that even pots and pans were hard to come by. Some families went to various settlements to carve out a land-based community for themselves.

The St. Paul des Métis colony was established in 1896 by the Oblate Fathers to provide a land base for impoverished Métis people. They hoped to obtain farm equipment from the government as well so that families might make a good start. There were thirty families reported there by Father Lacombe by October 1896. Amongst them, there were only a few Callihoos including Michel Callihoo's daughter's sons, Beauregards, the Boudreaus, and a Felix Callihoo. The Oblates also wanted the government to build an industrial school. When this didn't come off, they built a small private school anyway, depleting the meagre funds earned by the Colony's sawmill operation. Seed and implements were not immediately forthcoming, either. When the people finally planted some crops, the weather didn't always cooperate. When the government indicated that the

---

In the lobby of the Alberta Legislature is a bronze plaque which reads: "John Callihoo 1882–1957, born of Cree/Iroquois parents on the Michel Reserve. John Callihoo devoted his life to the welfare of his people, although often ignored by government officials and criticized for his work, he brought the Indians together as an active political force in the 1930s. This resulted in the forming of the Indian Association of Alberta in 1939 with Mr. Callihoo serving as president until 1947. He brought about many improvements in conditions on Indian Reserves in health, education and welfare services. This plaque was erected by the Indian Association of Alberta."[18]

land was wanted for French-Canadian settlers, some Métis moved away, weakening the community and the Oblates also became less tenacious in their efforts to keep it going. As time went on French-Canadian squatters took some of the lands, and even bought up the pews in church forcing many Métis to stand at the back. They found it easier than the Métis to borrow money for farm equipment from the banks. Frank Oliver provided a plan for the Federal Government to make grants of land to certain of the Métis and to deny the claims of others. The Colony was wound up by 1909. The last straw was that those whose claims had been disallowed were subtly prevented from lining up at the Land Office to apply for a homestead.[78]

In the 1930s a number of Métis Settlements were established. Some of them are still in existence as Métis communities. They came under the Métis Population Betterment Act of 1938 that was essentially a cooperative venture between the Government of Alberta and the Settlement Associations. Of course there were all sorts of controls devised by the ministry responsible, but the families were given economic assistance in addition to the designated lands. Many relatives and connections of the Callihoos have been contributing members of these communities for generations.

Roderick And Alice Callihoo

Roderick Callihoo, the last Chief, was born in 1917, on the Michel Reserve, a son of Johnny Callihoo and Sophie Cunningham. Sophie was another daughter of James Cunningham and Mary Hodgson. Roderick was educated at the convent in St. Albert. In 1939, he and his cousin Alice Labonte were married at the church in Villeneuve and settled down with his parents on the farm. Alice's father, Fred, was descended from an American immigrant family and her mother, Madeline, was James Callihoo's daughter. Roderick and Alice soon had a place of their own and ended up raising fifteen children. By this time, many women gave birth in hospital, but there was so much to do at home! It's a good thing that Alice wasn't afraid of hard work. During the Depression, from the age of twelve on she had to live away from home, doing housework and caring for other people's children for $10.00 per month plus board.

In 1948, Roderick was elected Chief, a post he kept until enfranchisement in 1958. During this time, the family moved to Edmonton where Roderick tried to make a living as a carpenter but they soon moved back to live the on the Reserve. They made their home in the abandoned school house and later built a new home, where they remained until 1966. The children were bused to school where their mother says they suffered from racial discrimination. The problems of a farmer hadn't changed. Roderick needed capital to make a success of this business. He believed that he, too, suffered discrimination when banks refused to lend him money. Roderick and Alice moved to St. Albert where Roderick died in 1980. He is buried in the cemetery there beside one of his sons.

Fred Labonte and Madeline Callihoo (1897–?) had the following children: Alice Malvina (1921–); Keith; Howard; Louise; James (1928–1998); Margaret; Emily; Edith; Edward; Eli (1935–1971)

Roderick and Alice had the following children: Donald Joseph (1940–); Carol Leona Marie (1942–; Dennis Patrick; James Louis; Dianne Beatrice; Rabdolph; Brian Neil Anthony; Ian Larry; Michael Edward; Roland; Sheila Roseanne; Donna; Constance.

Plate 24. Roderick and Alice Calahoo, Villeneuve, 1939
courtesy Jessie Callihoo

Plate 25. Oldest house left on Michel Reserve, built by Jim Callihoo, ca. 1910 *photo Elizabeth Macpherson*

Musical Talent

There are a number of famous fiddlers in the Callihoo family. Michel's sons, Solomon, Johnny and James, were great fiddlers as were grandsons Richard, Isidor and Norbert. Michel's youngest daughter, Emmaline, played a number of instruments. A grandnephew, Victor, and three other men made up the "Pioneers' Orchestra" consisting of two guitars and two fiddles. They played on the radio between hockey games for $1.50. To this day, Michel's great grandson, Gilbert Anderson, carries on the tradition and Michel's granddaughter, Beatrice Callihoo, is a well-known pianist and organist in Edmonton. Dancing used to be a most popular form of entertainment. Dances were held in small community centres where small bands including piano, fiddle, and guitar would play the popular music of the day as well as traditional Métis music. Church picnics were also very popular and had the added virtue of including everyone in the parish.

Today

This story is not yet over. The vitality and intelligence we saw in Louis Callihoo, the fur trade adventurer, persisted in his son Michel as he dealt with the many changes of the nineteenth century. He always made a living, raised a large family, and negotiated with the Government of his day. Subsequent generations of Callihoos have successfully coped with new forms of education, technology and politics, overcoming prejudice and poverty.

Modern Callihoos and their relatives participate in all aspects of society. Many have attended University; for example, Beatrice Callihoo's daughter Sheralyn has a Ph.D. and is a professor. Paul Callihoo's daughter Carmen is studying to be a park warden and his son, Dennis, is a lawyer. Paul Mitchell works for the City of St. Albert. Gilbert Anderson's son, Gilbert, is an opera singer. Peter Calliou is a Native activist. All the Callihoos I have talked to are very proud of their Aboriginal heritage.

BIBLIOGRAPHY

1. Anderako, Mark, 1985. *Historic Trails of Alberta.* Lone Pine, Edmonton, 160 pp.
2. Anderson, Anne, 1985. *The First Metis... A New Nation.* UVISCO Press, Edmonton, 494 pp.
3. Andrews, Gerry, 1985. *Métis Outpost.* Victoria, B.C., 340 pp.
4. Baergen, William Peter, 1967. *The Fur Trade at Lesser Slave Lake.* University of Alberta M.A. thesis, 209 pp.
5. Bellerose, Robert, 1977. *Transcript of interview by St. Albert Historical Society.* Musée Héritage Museum
6. Borgstede, Arlene, ed, 1985. *The Black Robe's Vision A History of St. Albert & District.* St. Albert Historical Society, 408 pp.
7. Bossauge, Corpl. G.H.L., 1889. *Diary, Northwest Mounted Police "G" Division.* Ms Glenbow Archives
8. Buchanan, D. & J.M. McIntyre, 1954. *The Descendants and Contemporaries of Louis l'Iroquois: Consanguinity and Two Rare Matings.* Ms Provincial Archives of Alberta
9. Calihoo, Robert & Robert Hunter, 1982. *Occupied Canada.* McClelland & Stewart Inc., Toronto, 271 pp.
10. Callihoo, Victoria, 1953. *Early Life in Lac Ste-Anne and St. Albert In the 1870s.* Alberta Historical Review Vol. 1, No. 3, p.21–26
11. ——1956. *Our Buffalo Hunts.* Alberta Historical Review Vol. 8, No. 1, p.24–25
12. Calverley et al. ed., 1982. *The Monkman Pass and Trail A Brief History.* Petro-Canada Coal Division 62 pp.
13. Carter, W.J. n.d. Forword p.1-5, Early Transportation, p.1–7 *Forty Years in the North West.* Ms University of Alberta, Special Collections.
14. Chalmers, John W., 1977. *Treaty No. Six.* Alberta History Vol 25, No. 2, p.22–27
15. ——1981. *Laird of the West.* Detsileg, Calgary, 289 pp.

16. Cheadle, Walter B., 1931. *Cheadle's Journal of a Trip across Canada, 1862–63*. Hurtig Ltd., Edmonton, 311 pp.

17. Coues, Elliot, ed., 1897. *New light on the Early History of the Greater Northwest: The Manuscript Journals of Alexander Henry and of David Thompson*. 3 vols. reprint 1965 Ross and Haines, Minneapolis, 1027 pp.

18. Cox, Ross, 1832. *The Columbia River.* Vol. 2 Colburn and Bentley, London, 350 pp.

19. Dalheim, Mrs. K & Mrs. M. Kerr ed., 1977. *Calahoo Trails*. Calahoo Women's Institute, 300 pp.

20. Davidson, G.C., 1918. *The Northwest Company*. Publications in History, Vol. VII U. of Calf. Press, Berkeley, 349 pp.

21. Dempsey, Hugh A., 1986. *The Indian Tribes of Alberta*. Glenbow Museum, Calgary, 100 pp.

22. —— 1986. *Gentle Persuader, biography of James Gladstone, Indian Senator.* Western Producer Prairie Books, 225 pp.

23. Department of Indian Affairs Public Archives of Canada
Black Series:
RG10: i. *3616/4518*, ii. *3768*, iii. *3670/10771*, iv. *3655/9000*,
v. *3665/10080*, vi. *3685/12932-3*, vii. *3707/19229-2*,
viii. *3809/53828-2*, ix. *3794/46205*, x. *3763/32594*,
xi. *3785/41783-4*, xii. *3809/53828-2*, xiii. *3836/67091*,
xiv. *3860/82319-8*, xv. *3868/87976*, xvi. *3907/106041*,
xvii. *3563/82 pt.14*, xviii. *3940/121698-10*, xix. *3843/72659-8*,
xx. *37790/33711*
xxi. RG:15 *Scrip Application Records, 1885, 1886, 1892, 1900, 1901* Provincial Archives of Alberta 90.562
xxii. *Annual Report of the Department of Indian Affairs 1903*, p.211.
xxiii. *Annual Report of the Department of Indian Affairs 1915*, p.79

24. Devine, E. J., 1922. *Historic Caughnawaga*. Messanger Press, Montreal, 443 pp.

25. Dion, Joseph F., 1979. *My Tribe the Crees*. Glenbow Museum, Calgary, 194 pp.

26. Drouin, Emeric, 1973. *Lac Ste-Anne Sakahigan.* Editions de l'Hermitage, Edmonton, 98 pp.

27. *Edmonton Bulletin*, 1881: March 28, October 29; 1882: January, April 15, June 10; 1883: June 2, March; 1885: April 23, June 13, November 14; 1886: August 21; 1887: March; 1888: February 25; 1895: April 14, October; 1897: August; 1898: August 13, October 27, December 1.

28. Ferris, Warren Angus, 1940. *Life in the Rocky Mountains. A Diary of Wanderings on the sources of the Rivers Missouri, Columbia, and Colorado from February, 1830, to November, 1835.* ed. Paul C. Phillips Rosenstock, The Old West Publishing Co., Denver, 365 pp.

29. Frisch, Jack A., 1976. *Some Ethnological and Ethnohistoric Notes on the Iroquois in Alberta.* Man in the Northeast, No. 12, p.51–64

30. Goyette, Linda, 1995. *Frank Oliver's Misadventures in Indian Country.* Edmonton Journal, June 1995, p.A9.

31. Gray Nuns, 1859–1915. *Chroniques des Soeurs Grises Vol. 1.* transcript Provincial Archives of Alberta 71.220/4242 B100

32. Grouard, E., 1923. *Souvenirs de mes soixante ans d'apostolat dans l'Athabasca-Mackenzie.* Librairie Catholique, Lyon-Paris, 440 pp.

33. Gunn, Hon. Donald, & Tuttle, Charles R., 1880. *History of Manitoba from the earliest Settlement.* McLean, Roger & Co., Ottawa

34. Harmon, D.W., 1811. *A journal of Voyages and Travels in the Interior of North America.* Courier Press, Toronto, 382 pp.

35. Hart, Hazel, 1980. *Gateway to the Rockies History of Hinton.* 352 pp.

36. Heidenreich, Conrad E. and Arthur J. Ray, 1976. *The Early Fur Trades: a study in cultural interaction.* McClelland and Stewart, Toronto, 95 pp.

37. Horstman, Louise & David May, eds., 1982. *Tired of Rambling: a history of Fishing Lake Métis Settlement.* Alberta Federation of Métis Settlement Associations, 69 pp.

38. Hudson's Bay Company
    i. *Edmonton Post Accounts, Hudson's Bay Company Archives,* B60/d/68, B60/d/71, B60/d/75a, B60/d/78a, B60/d/83, B60/d/90-93, B60/d//99, B60/d/107 and Fort Edmonton Park transcripts from Hudson's Bay Company Archives 1860–61, 1862–64, 1865–1866, 1869–71

ii. *Fort Assiniboine Journal, Hudson's Bay Company Archives,* B8/a/1

iii. *Fort Dunvegan Journal* Fort Edmonton Park, photocopy, 56/a/2, B56/a/7

iv. *Lesser Slave Lake Hudson's Bay Company Archives,* B115/a/1-9, B60/d/65, B60/d//68, B60/d/71, B115/z/1

v. *Fort Vermilion Journal Hudson's Bay Company Archives,* B224/a/5

vi. *York Factory Hudson's Bay Company Archives,* B.239/z/10, B.239/g/1-60, B.239/u/3, B239/d/237, B239/d/580, B239/d/610, B239/d/620, B239/d/621, B239/d/642.

vii. *Hudson's Bay Company Archives.* Biographical sheet copy in letter dated 3 November, 1995

39. Johnson, Alice M. ed., 1967. *Saskatchewan Journals and Correspondence.* Edmonton House 1795–1800, Chesterfield House 1800–1802. Hudson Bay Record Society, London, 26 pp.

40. Kane, Paul, 1859. *Wanderings of an artist among the Indians of North America, from Canada to Vancouver's Island and Oregon through the Hudson's Bay company's territory and back again.* Longman, Brown, Green, Longman and Roberts, London, 455 pp.

41. Klyne, Michael, 1827. *Jasper Post Journal.* Hudson Bay Company Archives, B.94/a/1

42. Lacombe Albert. n.d., *Memoirs.* Ms English translation. Provincial Archives of Alberta, 71.220/6575

43. —1864. *Notice Historique sur les Missions du Lac Ste- Anne, de St-Joachim, et de St-Albert 1842–1864.* Ms Provincial Archives of Alberta, 71.220/5441/123

44. —*Codex historicus, 1852–1872.* Provincial Archives of Alberta, 71.220/4213/99

45. Legal, Emile J., *Short Sketches of the History of the Catholic Churches and Missions in Central Alberta.* 174 pp.

46. MacDonald, George Heath, 1954. *Fort Augustus – Edmonton, Northwest Trails and Traffic.* Douglas Printing & McDermid Studios, Edmonton, 255 pp.

47. MacGregor, J.G., 1974. *Overland by the Yellowhead.* Western Producer Prairie Books, 270 pp.

48. ——1978. *John Rowand Czar of the Prairies.* Western Producer Prairie Books, 184 pp.

49. Mackenzie, Alexander, 1801. *Voyages from Montreal on the River St. Lawrence through the Continent of North America to the Frozen and Pacific Oceans.* R. Noble, London, 412 pp.

50. MacRae, A.O., 1912. *History of the Province of Alberta.* The Western Canada History Company (2V.)

51. McCardle, Bennet Ellen, 1982. *Indian History and Claims: a Research Handbook.* DIAND (2 V.).

52. Merk, Frederick, ed., 1931. *Fur Trade and Empire George Simpson's Journal.* Harvard University Press, Cambridge, 370 pp.

53. Masson, L.F.R., 1889. *Les Bourgeois de la Compagnie du Nord-Ouest.* De l'imprimerie General A. Cote et Cie. Quebec (Vol. 1)

54. Moberly, Henry John, 1929. *When Fur Was King.* J.M. Dent & Sons Ltd., London & Toronto, 237 pp.

55. Moodie, Donald Wayne, 196.5 *The St. Albert Settlement: A study in Historical Geography.* Ms U. of A. Ms. thesis, 179 pp.

56. Morris, Alexander, 1880. *The Treaties of Canada with the Indians of Manitoba and the North-West Territories.* Belfords, Clarke, Toronto, p.285–297 & p.365

57. Morton, Arthur S. ed., 1929. *The Journal of Duncan McGillivray of the North West Company at Fort George on the Saskatchewan, 1794–5.* MacMillan, Toronto

58. ——1938. *A History of the Canadian West to 1870–71.* Thomas Nelson and Sons Ltd., Toronto, 987 pp.

59. ——1944. *Sir George Simpson: overseas governor of the Hudson's Bay Company: a pen picture of a man of action.* Binfords-Mort for the Oregon Historical Society Portland, Oregon, 310 pp.

60. Nicks, Gertrude, 1969. *The Archaeology of Two Hudson's Bay Posts: Buckingham House (1792–1800) & Edmonton House III (1810–1813).* Thesis University of Alberta

61. ——1974. *History of Native Peoples of the Grande Cache Area.* Project Report Submitted to the Native Area Development Committee at Grande Cache, Alberta

62. ——1979. *Iroquois fur trappers and their descendants in Alberta. Origins of the Alberta Metis: Land Claims Research Project, 1978–1979*. ed. Pat and Joe Sawchuk. Metis Association of Alberta, Edmonton, p.17–34.

63. ——1980. *Demographic Anthropology of Native Populations in Western Canada, 1800–1975*. PhD diss. University of Alberta, 212 & 14pp.

64. ——1980. *Iroquois and the fur trade in western Canada In Old Trails And New Directions: Papers of the Third North American Fur Trade Conference*. ed. Carol Judd and Arthur Ray. University of Toronto Press, Toronto, p.85–101

65. ——1985. *The historic development of an indigenous Métis population*. pp.163–181 in Peterson, Jacqueline and Jennifer S.H. Brown ed. *The New Peoples: Being and Becoming Metis in North America*. University of Manitoba Press

66. ——1988. *Louis Callihoo*. p.137 In Dictionary of Canadian Biography, Volume VII, 1836–50. University of Toronto Press, Toronto

67. Northwest Company
 Northwest Company Servants Contracts:
 i. Hudson's Bay Company Archives, F.4/32, F.5/1 F.5/2, F5/3, B.239/g/61–65, 67–69, 70
 ii. *List of Men at Athabasca, 1805*. British Columbia Archives, A/B/20/N81
 iii. *James McKenzie Journal 1799–1800*. transcript British Columbia Archives, A/B/40/M19

68. Oblates of Mary Immaculate, Records of the Order
 i. *Codex historicus, Riviere Qui Barre 1886–1889*. (Father A. Blanchet) Provincial Archives of Alberta, 71.220/5383
 ii. *Codex historicus, Saint-Albert 1875–1884*. (Father Lacombe) Provincial Archives of Alberta, 71.220/5442
 iii. *Codex historicus, Saint-Albert 1889–1895*. Provincial Archives of Alberta, 71.220/7085
 iv. *Codex historicus, Saint-Albert 1884–1889*. Provincial Archives of Alberta, 71.220/5443

v. *Codex historicus du pèlerinage et documents a l'égard des premiers pèlerinages, 1889–1899, Lac Ste-Anne.* Provincial Archives of Alberta, 71.220/4214

vi. *Ecole Dunbow, Journal Quotidien, 1884–1922.* Provincial Archives of Alberta, 71.220/3380-3414

vii. *Liber animarum, Fort des Prairies, 1842–1895.* Provincial Archives of Alberta, 71.220/5218

viii. *Liber animarum, Lac Ste-Anne.* Provincial Archives of Alberta, 71.220/4208

ix. *Livre de comptes, Saint-Albert, 1868–1875.* Provincial Archives of Alberta, 71.220/7086

x. *Livre de comptes #1, Saint-Albert, 1873–1881.* Provincial Archives of Alberta, 71.220/5465

xi. *Livre de comptes #2, Saint-Albert, 1882–1886.* Provincial Archives of Alberta, 71.220/5466

xii. *Livre de comptes #2, Saint-Albert, 1883–1917.* Provincial Archives of Alberta, 71.220/5464

xiii. *Livre de comptes #3, Saint-Albert, 1887–1892.* Provincial Archives of Alberta, 71.220/5467

xiv. *Registres des baptêmes, Mariages et Sépultures, Fort des Prairies: 1842–1859, 1842–1851, 1844–1859, 1842–1888, 1842–1856, 1865–1874.* Provincial Archives of Alberta, 71.220/5213–5217

xv. *Registres des baptêmes Mariages et Sépultures, St-Albert, 1908–1911.* Provincial Archives of Alberta, 71.220/7083

69. Ockley, B.A., 1932. *A History of Early Edmonton.* M.A. thesis University of Alberta, 133 pp.

70. Palliser, John, 1863. *The Journal, Detailed Reports, and Observations Relative to the Exploration by Captain John Palliser of that portion of British North America, which in latitude lies between the British Boundary Line and the Height of Land or Watershed of the Northern or Frozen Ocean, Respectively and in Longitude, Years 1857, 1858, 1859 and 1860.* Printed by G.E. Eyre and W. Spottiswoode for H.M.S.O., London, 325 pp.

71. Parker, James McPherson, 1987. *Emporium of the North Fort Chipewyan and the Fur Trade to 1835*. Alberta Culture and Multiculturalism/Canadian Plains Research Center, University of Regina, 208 pp.

72. Pearce, William C., 1884. *Claims to land at St. Albert under the provisions of the Dominion Lands Act*. Ms. William Pearce Collection, Books and Records Collection, University of Alberta

73. Quebec Government, Archives Nationales, 1944. *Rapport de L'Archiviste pour 1943–1944*. Redempti Paradis Imp. Roi, 482 pp.

74. Ray, Arthur J., 1976. *Diffusion of Diseases in the Western Interior of Canada, 1830–1850*. The Geographical Review, April, p.139–157

75. Robertson, Collin, 1939. *Correspondence Book September 1817 to September 1822*. Champlain Society, Toronto, 372 pp.

76. Rundle, R.T., 1977. *The Rundle Journals, 1840–1848*. intro. and notes G.M. Hutchison, ed. Hugh Dempsey, Calgary, 414 pp.

77. *Saskatchewan Herald*, 7 Oct., 1878

78. Sawchuk, Sawchuk & Ferguson, 1981. *Metis Land Rights in Alberta A Political History Metis Association of Alberta*. 264 pp.

79. Smet, Pierre-Jean de in Chittenden, H.M. and A.T. Richardson, eds., 1905. *Life, Letters and Travels of Father Pierre John DeSmet, S.J., 1801–1873*. 4 vols. Francis P. Harper, New York

80. Smoky Historical Society, 1980. *Wagon Trails Grown Over Sexsmith to the Smoky*. 1190 pp.

81. Spaulding, Kenneth A., 1956. *Alexander Ross, The Fur Hunters of the Far West*. University of Oklahoma, Norman, Okla. p.194–5

82. Spry, Irene, ed., 1963. *The Palliser Expedition*. MacMillan Co., Toronto, 310 pp.

83. Supreme Court of the Northwest Territories, *Calleo vs Bellerive*. Provincial Archives of Alberta, 69.305/1431

84. —— *Fairchild Co. Ltd. vs Poirier et al.* Provincial Archives of Alberta, 69.305/4311

85. Taylor, John Leonard, 1985. *Treaty 6 (1876): Treaty Research Report*. DIAND, Ottawa

86. Tyler and Wright, 1978. *The Alienation of Indian Reserve Lands During the Administration of Sir Wilfrid Laurier 1896-1911.* Ms

87. Voorhis, Ernest, 1930. *Historic forts and trading posts of the French régime and of the English fur trading companies.* Compiled for Natural Resources Intelligence Service, Dept. of the Interior, Ottawa, 188 pp.

88. Wallace, W. Stewart ed., 1934. *Documents relating to the NorthWest Company.* Champlain Society, Toronto

89. White, M. Catherine ed., 1950. *David Thompson's Journals relating to Montana and Adjacent Regions 1808–1812.* Montana State University Press, Missoula, Montana, 345 pp.

90. Women's Institute, Onoway Branch ed. Elizabeth Turnbull, 1978. *The Pathfinders. A History of Onoway, Bilby, Brookdale, Glenford, Goldthorphe, Heatherdown, Hillcrest, Nakumun, Rich Valley, Speldhurst, Stettin and Sturgeon River.* p.351–354

91. Wright, Richard and Rochelle, 1974. *Yellowhead Mileposts Route of the Overlanders.* Mitchell Press Vol 1, 251 pp.

Index